THE
VANISHING
FEAST

DOROTHY HINSHAW PATENT

THE VANISHING FEAST

*How Dwindling Genetic Diversity
Threatens the World's Food Supply*

A GULLIVER GREEN BOOK
HARCOURT BRACE & COMPANY
San Diego   New York   London

Copyright © 1994 by Dorothy Hinshaw Patent
Gulliver Green is a registered trademark of Harcourt Brace & Company.

All rights reserved. No part of this publication
may be reproduced or transmitted in any form or by
any means, electronic or mechanical, including photocopy,
recording, or any information storage and retrieval system,
without permission in writing from the publisher.

Requests for permission to make copies
of any part of the work should be mailed to:
Permissions Department, Harcourt Brace & Company,
6277 Sea Harbor Drive, Orlando, Florida 32887-6777.

Library of Congress Cataloging-in-Publication Data
Patent, Dorothy Hinshaw.
The vanishing feast/Dorothy Hinshaw Patent.
p. cm.—"A Gulliver Green Book"
ISBN 0-15-292867-7
1. Crops—Germplasm resources—Juvenile literature.
2. Livestock—Germplasm resources—Juvenile literature.
3. Germplasm resources—Juvenile literature.
4. Biological diversity conservation—Juvenile literature.
5. Agriculture—Juvenile literature. [1. Biological diversity.
2. Conservation of natural resources. 3. Agriculture.]
I. Title. II. Series.
S494.3.P38 1994
338.1'62—dc20 94-2227

The text was set in Deepdene.

Gulliver Green® Books focus on various aspects of ecology and the
environment, and a portion of the proceeds from the sale of these books
will be donated to protect, preserve, and restore native forests.

This book was printed using soya-based inks on acid-free,
recycled-content paper containing more than 10 percent postconsumer waste.

Designed by Linda Lockowitz
Printed in the United States of America
First edition

A B C D E

For all those who
strive to provide healthy food
for the world's people in the most
environmentally responsible
ways possible

ACKNOWLEDGMENTS

The author wishes to thank
John Bender of Mokelumne River Ranch,
the American Livestock Breeds Conservancy,
and the USDA for their help with this book.
Abundant thanks are also due my editor,
John Radziewicz, who has helped guide me
in the creation of three books, all of which
have been immeasurably improved
by his input.

CONTENTS

Contents

INTRODUCTION

Living things on earth, whether wild species, domesticated animals, or crop plants, are in a constant evolutionary race for survival. When a new disease emerges, its host must respond with new defenses or risk extinction. Plants and animals must also be well adapted to the physical elements of the environments in which they live—temperature, rainfall, and so on. The ways in which organisms react to environmental challenges are controlled by their genes, the units of heredity that produce their physical traits. For example, some genes make organisms susceptible to disease and other genes confer resistance. Over time, both wild and cultivated species living in difficult environmental conditions and exposed to various diseases have evolved abundant genetic variations that help them persevere.

Because humans rely on plants and animals for food, preserving the genetic variability of the species that feed us is critical to our own survival. Yet dramatic changes in agricultural systems around the world during the second half of the twentieth century have resulted in alarming decreases in the genetic diversity we depend on.

What are those changes? How have they decreased

diversity? What roles has genetic variation played in helping to improve our crops and domesticated animals, and how can it be used in the future? How can we protect the diversity that exists today?

This book explores what diversity can do for us, how it is threatened, and what we can do to preserve it. The topic of genetic diversity is of critical importance. We are approaching the twenty-first century with an ever-increasing human population that needs to be fed. At the same time, an increasingly monolithic agricultural industry relies more and more on genetic uniformity rather than on genetic diversity to solve the problem of how to feed that population. Fortunately, ways exist to safeguard our heritage of valuable diversity. But we must educate ourselves, plan ahead, and make compromises in order to succeed.

PART 1

WHY DIVERSITY?

WHAT IS DIVERSITY?

I t was the winter of 1942, in the middle of World War II. The Germans were shelling Leningrad, Russia. No food could come in to feed the people, and there was no heat. Tens of thousands were dying from the cold and starvation. D. S. Ivanov was one of the casualties. But Ivanov was different from most of those who perished. At his death, he was surrounded by thousands of packets of rice—rice too precious to eat, even if it meant saving his own life. Ivanov was not the only one to die at the All Union Research Institute of Plant Industry. One of his colleagues died at his writing table, working until the last moment, while others starved slowly, protecting boxes of corn, wheat, peas, and other edible seeds. Altogether, ten dedicated workers starved at the institute in the process of saving the world's greatest collection of seeds and tubers.

The Strengths of Diversity

The curators in Leningrad during World War II, at what is now called the Vavilov Institute, were willing to die to save seeds and tubers because they knew the collection held the future strength of Russian agriculture and perhaps that of the entire world as well. They understood that without an abundance of variety to choose from, the farms that feed the world's people could easily fall victim to any of a number of devastating problems—diseases that destroy crops, climates that restrict what can be grown, or inad-

---

Previous page: While it may seem that we eat an abundant variety of food, we actually depend on a limited variety of only a few foods for our survival. PHOTO COURTESY OF USDA

equate yields of the basic foods people depend on for survival.

Diversity in the foods we eat isn't a topic that crosses our minds. We decide to make a meal of steak, potatoes, sliced tomatoes, and corn, with apple pie for dessert, without realizing that each component of our meal can exhibit dazzling variety. That steak could come from breeds of cattle that thrive in the moderate summers and harsh winters of Montana or from other kinds that do best in the hot, humid summers and mild winters of Texas. Because potatoes exist in so much variety, they can grow in just about any agricultural climate in the world, from the cool lowlands of Holland to the hot, humid plains of India or the highlands of Peru, where frost is an almost nightly occurrence. Tomatoes, corn, and apples also come in hundreds of different forms—most of which we never see—each adapted to the environment where it is grown. Because our foods possess great variety, agriculturalists have been able to mold nature into strains of plant and animal foods that produce abundantly, resist diseases, and bear crops or produce meat and dairy products wherever humans live.

Changes over Time

Genetics and evolution help explain how differences in living things come about, how they are passed from one generation to the next, and why they are important. The basic physical characteristics of any organism are determined by the genes located on the chromosomes in each cell. The genes direct cell activities and thus determine the characteristics of the organism. Among plants such as corn, for example, traits including the size and color of its seed, the height of its stalks, the earliness or lateness of crop production, as well as its resistance to different diseases, are all carried by the genes.

The chromosomes are found in the cell nucleus and come in pairs. One chromosome in each pair comes from the female parent and one comes from the male parent. Every time a cell divides, the chromosomes, along with their array of genes, are copied so that each cell in any organism has an identical set of genes.

When organisms reproduce sexually (in flowering plants, by way of pollen from the male parent pollinating the stigma, or female part of the flower; in animals, through sperm from the male fertilizing eggs from the female) the chromosomes behave differently. The two chromosomes of each pair come together and may exchange pieces, a process called crossing-over. Then, as the cell divides to form eggs and sperm, only one chromosome from each pair goes to each egg or sperm cell. When pollination or fertilization occurs, the resulting fertilized egg will have one chromosome in each pair from the male parent and one from the female. This makes it different from either parent. The process of shuffling genes through crossing-over and sexual reproduction is called genetic recombination.

The genes are also copied just before the egg and sperm cells are produced. Sometimes a mistake is made during this copying, and the gene is not reproduced exactly. These errors, called mutations, are the real stuff of evolution. Mutations can alter any sort of trait, some you can see and others you can't. Many mutations are fatal, but those that are not allow species to change and adapt over time. Because of mutations, genes evolve into different forms, called alleles.

A mutation can change the texture of an animal's hair, for example, so that one allele produces straight hair while another results in a curly coat. Other mutations can alter an important chemical component of the organism, changing the temperature range in which it functions best. Depending on which genes they affect, mutations can result in myriad variations in the appearance or functioning of the organism. Some changes brought about by mutations are so subtle that their effects seem invisible; others are obvious.

The differential survival of individuals carrying particular alleles plus the recombination of traits from the male and female parents lead to the kinds of individual variation we can see in any type of plant or animal. Just look at the members of a human family. One person may have blond hair and blue eyes, while his sister has brown hair and brown eyes. His brother may be several inches taller than he is, even though they have both been well fed all their lives. The list of differences could go on and on.

In wild plants and animals, the individuals that are best adapted to their environment are most likely to survive to reproduce, making the alleles they carry more prevalent in the next generation. Through this process of evolutionary adaptation over many generations, wild species become progressively better adapted to the environmental conditions in which they live. Consider wild tomatoes. Tomatoes are native to western South America, Central America, and Mexico. Each one of the eight to ten wild tomato species is adapted to different conditions. Some grow at low elevations, where they are subjected to hot temperatures and a variety of diseases. Others, however, live at higher altitudes and have to cope with cold nighttime temperatures and short growing seasons. The array of genes carried by each of these tomato species allows it to survive and reproduce in its environment. That assortment of genes is different from what is found in the other species, each of which is adapted to a different environment. A highland tomato species might quickly perish from disease in a lowland environment, while a lowland species would die at a touch of frost if planted in the highlands.

Individuals within a species vary from one another as well. Some plants may grow taller than others, and some may bloom earlier or later. The wider the area over which a particular species lives, the more variation it encounters in its environment and thus the greater the variation among individuals within that species. For these reasons, each wild species is a storehouse of genetic information.

Wild Gene Windfall

Wild tomatoes are an especially rich source of useful genes. When plant breeders strive to improve tomatoes and to develop strains that are adapted to specific environments, they can turn to wild relatives for genes that may confer the traits they are seeking. For example, one wild tomato species lives above an altitude of three thousand feet and can tolerate light frosts. Cultivated tomatoes, on the other hand, are killed by frost, making them chancy to grow in areas where frost hits in early fall. Plant breeders are working on incorporating the genes that enable this wild tomato to survive frost into the cultivated species. If they are successful, the length of the growing season for tomatoes could be greatly extended in northern and mountain regions.

Another wild tomato relative lives on the Galápagos Islands of Ecuador just above the high-tide line. It survives in soil that is moistened by pure seawater. Plant breeders have crossed this species with cultivated tomatoes to produce a plant with tasty cherry-tomato–size fruit that can tolerate 70 percent seawater. These plants will grow on land otherwise useless for crops because of the amount of salt in the soil or in areas where the only water available for irrigation comes from the sea.

Perhaps the most dramatic story of how an unpromising-looking wild plant can end up being useful is told by botanist Hugh Iltis. In 1962, Dr. Iltis and another scientist were in Peru, looking for evidence as to where wild potatoes were first gathered and bred into cultivated varieties. While collecting specimens in a beautiful Andean valley, Iltis noticed a ratty-looking wild tomato plant with yellow flowers and tiny green-and-white-striped berries. It didn't look much like a supermarket tomato. But the scientists had never seen this species before, so they were glad to find it. They smashed some of the fruits in newspaper to collect the seeds and sent them to Charles Rick, a tomato geneticist at the University of California, Davis.

Dr. Rick found this species, identified as N. 832, very interesting. He experimented with making crosses between N. 832 and a commercial tomato variety. This kind of research takes years of careful breeding, trying different

crosses among species and varieties to find promising combinations. By 1980, Dr. Rick had succeeded in producing
several new tomato varieties with big, brightly colored
fruits. The most important trait of these new tomatoes was
their low moisture content. Tomatoes are largely water—
most kinds have only 4.5 to 6.2 percent soluble solid matter. But through his crosses and selection, Dr. Rick
managed to produce tomatoes with as much as 7.5 percent
soluble solids. The more soluble solids in the fruit, the
better the flavor, and the more useful the fruit is for making products such as tomato paste and sauce. One expert
estimated that a mere 0.5 percent increase in soluble solids
would be worth a million dollars a year to the tomato
industry! Dr. Iltis's scrawny wild plant turned out to be
a gold mine potentially worth millions of dollars.

Valuing Wild Relatives

Wild animals related to domesticated species can be a valuable source of genes that may be used to improve livestock raised on farms and ranches. Like cultivated plants,
all domesticated animals were developed from wild species. As with plants, the traits humans value in animals
can be quite different from the characteristics of the wild
species. Wild sheep, for example, grow thick coats of fur
in fall for protection from winter's cold and then shed
them in the spring, leaving just a sleek coat of coarse hair.
Most domesticated sheep do not shed. They have been
selected for soft coats that continue to grow and are shorn
by people to produce wool.

Sheep provide people in Western countries primarily
with wool and only secondarily with meat. But more than

a billion sheep live worldwide, and in dozens of countries, sheep are a very important source of meat and milk. Domesticated sheep have their drawbacks. One reason sheep aren't very popular for food in Western countries is their strongly flavored meat. Sheep are also susceptible to a number of parasites and diseases. And most breeds of sheep typically give birth to just one lamb each spring, with twins somewhat common and triplets rare.

The wild relatives of sheep could help resolve these problems. The meat of wild sheep is tender and mild in flavor, making it more suitable to human taste than the strongly flavored mutton from domesticated sheep. Wild sheep are also resistant to a number of the diseases and parasites that can infest domesticated flocks. And the ewes of some wild sheep can produce more than twice the average number of lambs of most domesticated breeds. All these traits are influenced by the genetic heritage of the animals, so it might prove practical to incorporate them into domesticated breeds. Unfortunately, wild sheep numbers are decreasing because of habitat loss, indiscriminate hunting, and competition from their domesticated relatives. Some species are threatened with extinction and may die out before their potential for improving domesticated sheep is even tested.

CHAPTER TWO

THE PERILS
OF UNIFORMITY

The critical importance of the great genetic resources available in both domesticated and wild diversity emerges dramatically when crop plants are too inbred, becoming too much the same. Inbreeding—crossing organisms with close relatives and thereby decreasing the number of different alleles for their genes—can have disastrous consequences.

Tomatoes provide a recent, dramatic example. In 1993, a new virus carried by the tiny greenhouse whitefly attacked California tomato plants, which lack resistance to both the fly and the virus. The tomato industry in Orange County, which had sales of $17.4 million in 1992, lost about $2 million as a result. The most effective defense against the threat might be introducing genes that can resist the fly and/or virus into the susceptible commercial tomato varieties. But that would take years of research. In the meantime, scientists are carefully monitoring possible host plants of the fly and are looking for natural enemies that might attack it.

Starvation in Ireland

The Irish potato famine provides a powerful example of what can happen when a vital crop lacks genetic diversity. Potatoes are vulnerable to uniformity because they are usually grown by planting pieces of the tubers themselves rather than seeds. All the cells of the tubers have the same genetic composition as the rest of the plant, so reproduc-

---

The mule-footed hog, with its single fused hoof, might be useful in producing pigs that are better adapted to walking on concrete floors than are typical pigs with split hooves. PHOTO BY DOROTHY H. PATENT

13

tion by way of tubers does not result in genetic recombination. This means that each year's crop of potatoes will be just the same genetically as the previous. If there is some variability among the plants to start with, however, farmers can choose to plant tubers from the best-adapted plants. But without recombination of genes through sexual reproduction, crop improvement is restricted.

A limited variety of potatoes was brought from South America to Ireland in 1590. At first, these potatoes were poorly adapted to northern conditions. But through selection of tubers from plants that produced early and selection of seeds from desirable plants, European potatoes were improved. By the late eighteenth century, potatoes were becoming a major crop in Ireland.

Potatoes are a cheap, easy-to-grow food that is especially nutritious. Irish peasants quickly developed a dependence on potatoes for sustenance, consuming nine to fourteen pounds a day per person. The population of the country soared to over eight million, more than twice as many people as live there now. The population density was greater than that of China today.

Irish dependence on the potato was a ticking time bomb. Since only a limited number of tubers were initially introduced to Ireland, Irish potatoes had little genetic variability to start with. The selecting that had been done to enable early harvest and other desirable traits had limited their genetic diversity even more. In 1845, a deadly fungus disease of potatoes called late blight struck northern Ireland. The plants were completely defenseless against the onslaught. Tubers rotted in the ground, and those already harvested turned black and disintegrated. The terrible

14

blight spread quickly until the entire country was affected. By the time the famine ended in 1851, at least a million Irish had starved to death, and more than a million had emigrated to North America.

Ireland wasn't the only country affected. Potatoes throughout Europe suffered from the blight, but nowhere else as dramatically as in Ireland. Fortunately, a German breeder brought blight-resistant potatoes from Mexico to Europe in the mid-nineteenth century and used them to infuse some blight resistance into European potatoes. Since that time, resistance to blight has been a major goal in potato breeding. One of the best sources of genes that bring about that objective is a wild potato relative from South America. Through careful breeding, genes from this species have been introduced into the genetic constitution of potatoes almost everywhere the crop is grown.

Breeding for blight resistance eventually saved the day for Ireland, which continues to be one of the countries most dependent on potatoes. Without resistant varieties, the potato would have been lost as an important world food crop. And without potatoes, many northern countries would have difficulty feeding their millions of people.

Corn—A Critical Crop

Corn's efficiency at gathering sunlight and harnessing its energy to produce starches and sugars is unsurpassed in the plant world. Thanks to the work of breeders since the 1920s, corn has become the world's most efficient industrial crop. It feeds people and livestock all over the world. Right after the American Civil War (1866), corn yielded between twenty and thirty bushels per acre. That figure stayed quite stable until intensive breeding began in the 1930s. From then until the mid-1960s, the yield of corn increased to around eighty bushels per acre. By 1987, that figure had increased to 120 bushels per acre, more than a fourfold increase since Civil War times.

Corn is different from familiar flowering plants such as petunias and pansies that attract bees to their blossoms. The bees carry pollen from one flower to the next, pollinating the flowers as they collect sweet nectar. Such plants need only produce small amounts of pollen since the bees are very efficient at their job. Corn, however, is wind pollinated. Separate male and female flowers are produced on each plant. The male flowers, called tassels, grow near the tops of the stalks. The female flowers are borne on the cobs, hidden inside the tightly wrapped husks. The silks that protrude from the husks are sticky and trap the pollen, which then grows through the silks all the way to the female flowers and pollinates them. Wind pollination can be chancy, so corn produces huge amounts of pollen. One plant may release eighteen million separate tiny pollen grains! On a calm day, the pollen may land on the silks of the same plant. But on a windy day, corn pollen can travel long distances, even several miles.

The huge amount of pollen that corn produces creates problems for breeders. In their efforts to develop improved corn varieties, breeders select one strain of corn as the female parent and another as the male parent. Pollen from the male parent is used to pollinate the ears of the female parent. In order to control pollination, to make sure that the pollen the human breeder wants to use is the only pollen that reaches the ears, the tassels on each plant that will be a female parent must be removed by hand before the male flowers open and begin releasing their prodigious load of pollen. In the 1950s at the places where corn breeders developed new varieties, 125,000 workers had to be organized, trained, and supervised to do this work at a cost of about $10 million each year. Many college students helped pay for their educations by detasseling corn during their summer vacations.

During the 1950s, scientists discovered a genetic trait that made their work much easier. When present, the gene resulted in corn plants that produced no viable pollen. Breeders introduced this male-sterile gene into almost all the strains of corn used as female parents in their breeding programs so the plants wouldn't need detasseling. Countless hours of labor and the related costs were saved, and corn breeders were confident that from then on, their work would be easier.

It wasn't long before the mistake of putting the same gene in most corn varieties caught up with the breeders. In 1961, farmers in the Philippines began to warn of a problem with their corn crop. The plants seemed to be especially susceptible to a particular disease. No one paid much attention, even when the same disease was reported in Mexico. By 1968, what would eventually be called southern corn leaf blight was turning up here and there in the American Midwest. Still, no one seemed to take it seriously. By this time, breeders were relying so extensively on the male-sterile gene that up to 90 percent of corn grown commercially carried it.

In 1969, some Florida growers began to realize that the varieties they grew all seemed very susceptible to southern corn leaf blight. Corn is planted early in Florida, where the climate is mild, and the disease began showing up during February 1970 in the southern part of the state. Fortified by especially warm, humid weather, the blight spread its spores northward on the winds. By May, it was attacking the crop in Alabama and Mississippi. By mid-June, all three states faced a serious problem, and parts of Louisiana and Texas were also in trouble.

Southern corn leaf blight thrives in moist environments. When the spores land on the film of water coating a corn leaf, the disease attacks quickly. In one day, tan markings appear on the leaves, and within a few days, an entire field of corn can be devastated, the cobs crumbling into worthless bits after falling off the plants. Every ten days brings a new generation of the disease. By late June 1970 the blight was on its way to the midwestern Corn Belt. By that time it was too late to stop the disaster since the nation's entire corn crop had already been planted. Farmers were left to stand by and watch, hoping that their fields would be spared. By the end of the harvest, 15 percent of the American crop had failed, a loss of more than a billion bushels of corn. Southern states were especially hard hit, and many farmers in the South were put out of business.

The United States Department of Agriculture (USDA) was unaware of the grave danger. As late as August 1, it was predicting a bumper crop, even after much of America's corn had already been destroyed. Part of the reason for the USDA's lack of concern was that southern states regularly had trouble with blight of one sort or another. Difficulties in the South seemed of little concern since the midwestern states Illinois, Indiana, and Iowa accounted for half of the country's corn harvest. It was late August before the USDA admitted there was a serious problem.

Corn breeders also finally took notice, realizing that almost all commercial varieties of corn possessed the male-sterile gene, and that the gene made them susceptible to southern corn leaf blight. Fortunately, resistance to the disease was found in a strain of African corn, but because realization of the problem came so late, there was not enough resistant seed to go around in 1971. Corn growers were lucky that year: the weather was drier than in 1970, and the combination of some resistant corn and better weather kept losses to blight down in 1971. Meanwhile, breeders devoted their efforts to producing resistant seed, so that in 1972 there was an ample supply of resistant seed corn. The crisis was over.

Vulnerable Crops

Genetic uniformity plays an insidious role in the cultivation of many economically important world crops. During the colonial period of world history when European nations set sail to other parts of the world and conquered southern lands, the Europeans brought favored crops from one country to another for cultivation. In the process, just a few individuals of the species often constituted the entire founding stock. The original introduction of coffee to South America was from just one tree! In later years, genetic material from a few more plants was brought into South America. But even today, the coffee grown in South and Central America is dangerously lacking in genetic diversity, making the crop potentially susceptible to disease.

Palm oil, used in various foods, is an important product in some parts of Asia. Yet the entire Asian industry relies on plants derived from just four palm trees shipped to Indonesia in the mid-nineteenth century.

The degree of genetic diversity of the world's crops varies, but the trend is toward ever-increasing uniformity even in the most widely grown crops. In Indonesia 1,500 rice varieties disappeared over a recent five-year period, an average of three hundred varieties lost each year. And wherever uniformity prevails, farmers must use large amounts of pesticides and other chemicals to protect their crops, which costs them money and endangers their health.

Change Is the Only Constant

Are the world's potato and corn harvests now safe forever? The answer is emphatically *no*. The pests and diseases that plague our domesticated crops evolve over time. Just like the common cold that plagues humans, these harmful organisms keep coming back in different genetic guises that allow them to infect formerly resistant varieties of plants. The recent outbreak of the tomato virus carried by the whitefly is a dramatic illustration of such dynamic evolution. For this reason, plant breeders must constantly be on the lookout for new genes that can help plants resist infections and insect pests. The war with the late blight disease of potatoes continues, for example. During the 1930s, yet another strain of this disease hit European potato fields. Fortunately, however, a combination of still more genes from the wild species enabled the crop to survive the fungus attack with little damage.

Domesticated animals face many of the same problems as crop plants. When animals raised in crowded conditions are too inbred, diseases can sweep through and kill most of them. For example, domesticated turkeys raised for human consumption comprise only a few inbred strains. All of them are very susceptible to certain diseases such as blackhead, which can swiftly wipe out an entire flock. Turkey farmers have to be extremely careful around their animals to protect them from disease. They must step into pans of antiseptic solution before entering the barns where the animals live. If a turkey farmer visits a neighbor's farm, he or she must wear clean clothes, then change those clothes again before going into his or her own barns in case the neighbor's birds were infected.

The threat of pests and diseases is not the only reason for preserving the diversity of cultivated plants, domesticated animals, and their wild relatives. As we saw with tomatoes, genes from wild relatives can potentially expand the range over which a crop can be grown. Methods of raising crops or animals can change. In recent decades, apple farmers have been experimenting with a radically new method of raising apples. Instead of planting trees that grow ten feet or more in height and take several years to bear fruit, they have begun to plant truly miniature trees that grow only a few feet tall and that produce fruit within a year or two. These tiny trees are planted close together. Once they bear fruit, it is harvested by machine like corn or any other annual crop. In order to perfect this new system of growing apples, breeders needed to use genes that result in very small, early-yielding trees.

Uncommon breeds of animal can also be used to help

solve problems arising from the way domesticated animals are raised. For example, pigs are adapted to living on soft ground. Their hooves have two toes that can help them walk over uneven or soggy surfaces. But pigs today are raised on concrete floors, and they may have problems with their feet splaying out. A strange kind of pig, called the mule-footed hog, has one large toe instead of two smaller ones. Some people think that if the mule-footed trait were bred into commercially raised hogs, they would have fewer serious problems with their feet.

Genetic diversity in domesticated animals can also help livestock breeders adapt to the changing tastes of the public. Until the 1980s, people wanted to eat beef with "marbling," muscle fibers streaked with fat that makes meat tender and juicy. But then, as scientists discovered more about how animal fat and cholesterol in the diet can promote heart disease, the public came to prefer lean meat rather than the fatty, marbled kind. Animal breeders responded by working to produce American cattle with leaner carcasses that would appeal to the public's new tastes. To do so they imported breeds from other countries, such as the Italian Piedmontese, that can produce lean carcasses of tender meat.

For all these reasons—to keep ahead of pests and diseases in the evolutionary race; to extend the growing region of crops; to improve the quality of our crops and animal foods; to accommodate the changing conditions of crop cultivation and animal production; and to appeal to the shifting tastes of the public—it is important to maintain as much genetic diversity in our crop plants and domesticated animals as possible.

Corn is the only major world crop that began in North America—specifically, in Mexico. Corn is more properly called *maize*, a word derived from the native name for the grain. Actually a giant grass, maize is a cultivated plant, one that could never survive without humans. Normally, plants have ways of scattering their mature seeds, releasing them to germinate and form the next generation. But corn is different. Its seeds are always tightly bound to the cob. Not only that, the entire cob is enveloped in several layers of tough husk. Corn requires humans to free its seeds from the cob and plant them.

The story of the scientific effort to uncover corn's beginnings provides a particularly critical example of the need for preserving not only domesticated varieties of crops but also the places that harbor their wild relatives. No one knows for sure just how corn came into being, for details about its origins about ten thousand years ago are confused. For many years, some scientists believed that a wild grass called teosinte was an ancestor of maize. But this idea had a serious flaw. Each cell in the corn plant has just twenty chromosomes, while the annual teosinte familiar to science had forty. How could a plant with forty chromosomes be an ancestor to one with twenty? A big break for researchers interested in maize came in 1978. The American botanist Hugh Iltis was convinced that an unknown kind of teosinte was corn's true ancestor. He designed a Christmas card depicting his version of a teosinte once found in a part of Mexico but thought to be extinct. When a Mexican professor received Iltis's card, she dared her students to try to find the elusive plant; maybe it

Up Close:
THE WONDERFUL DIVERSITY OF CORN

was still out there somewhere in the wild. Rafael Guzman took her challenge seriously, spending his Christmas vacation searching for the supposedly extinct teosinte. In the mountains of southwestern Mexico, Guzman found some tall grass that looked as if it might be what he was looking for. He collected some seeds, which were sent to Iltis. Iltis planted them and was delighted by the results—each plant's cells had only twenty chromosomes, just like maize. Here was a newfound species, a perennial teosinte that lives on year after year. In contrast, corn and the other teosinte die out each season after producing seeds.

Because it has the same number of chromosomes as maize, the perennial teosinte can interbreed with it. Some scientists hail it as corn's only ancestor, claiming that selective breeding by early Americans turned teosinte into corn. But the two plants are very different. Teosinte has a brittle spike with six to twelve seeds, not a seed-laden cob. Each teosinte seed is separately wrapped in a case as hard as an acorn shell.

A number of major genetic changes would seem to be necessary to transform this small, naked spike of a few hard-shelled seeds into a well-wrapped cob of numerous bare seeds. Many scientists believe that cultivated corn derived from a cross between teosinte and a hypothetical type of wild corn and/or other ancestors. One corn expert, Paul Mangelsdorf, never accepted teosinte as a predecessor of maize. Until his death in 1989, Mangelsdorf believed that teosinte was actually derived from corn as a hybrid between it and an ancient type of popcorn called pod corn.

Genetic tests done in the late 1980s show that teosinte didn't need a great number of genetic changes to evolve into maize. Just a few genes—perhaps five—control the most important differences between the two plants. A number of less influential genes—probably a few dozen—refine the influence of the major genes to produce the familiar corn plant. Studies like this indicate that teosinte could well be corn's sole ancestor.

Whatever its origins, corn has become one of the most genetically diverse crop plants. From its origins in Mexico, maize spread south into what are now Bolivia and Peru, reaching even into the highlands of the Andes and the Amazon rain forest. To the east, corn spread to the Arawak and Carib tribes of the Antilles Islands. Woodland Indian tribes of the Mississippi and Ohio river valleys grew it, as did the Hopi and Navajo in the American Southwest. During the thousands of years maize has been cultivated by Native Americans, it has become exquisitely adapted to an impressive range of conditions and has developed a dizzying variety of forms. There is two-foot-tall corn and twelve-foot corn, corn with thumb-size ears and corn with eighteen-inch-long ears. Maize comes with white, yellow, red, black, and blue kernels, or in ears with all the colors mixed. Some corn grown in the north produces in only sixty days, while tropical varieties may require eleven months to mature.

The familiar sweet corn that we eagerly await in summertime is different from the majority of corn types. Most corn is starchy when ripe. As corn kernels form, sugars are deposited inside. This makes them sweet. But as the kernels mature, the sugar is turned to starch. The sweet corn that we eat straight off the cob or from packages out of the freezer has been selected so that the conversion of sugar to starch is partially blocked. That's what makes it sweet.

Maize is used for a variety of purposes, depending on the kind of starch it contains. About 80 percent of the corn grown in the United States today is called dent corn because the tops of the kernels are dented when dried. Most of that corn doesn't go to feed people—it fattens cattle and hogs before slaughter. Corn with hard kernels (flint corn) is good for making cornmeal, while kernels containing softer starch (flour corns) make the best corn flour. The hardest corn of all is popcorn. The outer starch of its kernels is very hard, while inside is a small amount of soft starch.

Corn is an ancient crop with almost infinite variety.

PHOTO BY DAVID CAVAGNARO

When the kernels are heated, the moisture in the soft starch turns to steam and expands, but the hard outside holds it in. When the pressure gets too great, the kernel explodes, producing puffy popcorn.

Within each type of maize are dozens to hundreds of individual varieties, each with its own special characteristics that determine the way it grows and the qualities of its kernels. Cornstarch, a thickener used in making pies and puddings, is an important corn product. Researchers recently tested starch from three hundred corn varieties and found ten with interesting new traits. One kind produces a clear gel, which can be used to replace more expensive thickeners such as tapioca. Another gives bakery products a velvety texture and retains moisture so that cakes will stay fresh longer.

Even when the kernels look alike, the corn can be very different. Hopi blue flour corn is superficially similar to Tarahumara blue flint corn from Chihuahua, Mexico. Both are even adapted to the same kinds of semiarid growing conditions. But they differ in many characteristics carried by their genes, such as the placement of the cobs on the stalks, the weight of the ears, and the number of days it takes for them to mature.

The importance of choosing varieties adapted to the growing region is clear with corn. Gary Nabhan, a scientist who devotes his life to preserving the diversity of Native American crops, planted some Hopi blue flour corn along with two types of closely related corn that was grown on the floodplains around Taos and Isleta pueblos in New Mexico. He also tested a popular, widely adapted modern variety called Golden Cross Bantam, since corn geneticists say such high-yielding "improved" varieties can do better than the native "unimproved" types even when conditions aren't especially good. Nabhan planted the seeds eight inches deep, the way the Hopi plant their blue corn, in very sandy soil; he watered the seeds once, then left them. Six days later, almost half the Hopi blue sprouts were poking their healthy green shoots above the surface. But fewer than a quarter of the other blue corn seedlings had emerged, and none of the Golden Cross Bantam ones were up. When he dug into the sand to see what had happened, Nabhan found that the Bantam plants didn't have a chance—their tender young leaves were all bent and curled under from the weight of the sand. He found that the Hopi seedlings had special adaptations for deep planting in sand. Their shoots grew almost ten inches in length, compared with the five inches of the Golden Cross Bantam seedlings. Deep planting allows the Hopi to get around the problems of growing corn in a dry, sandy region. Sandy soil doesn't hold water well, and deep planting puts the seeds far enough down so that their roots can find water.

As long as crops are grown in areas where native varieties grow better than modern "improved" ones, some diversity will be preserved by the people who rely on those crops for survival. The Hopi will always plant the special corn that can grow in the desert, and the Peruvians of the high Andes will continue to grow potatoes that will produce a harvest in that harsh land. But in areas where growing conditions are less severe, the temptation to substitute high-yielding, uniform varieties for the old, familiar ones is usually too great to resist.

CHAPTER THREE

PRESSURES
AGAINST PRESERVATION

Despite the obvious importance of preserving the wild relatives of domesticated plants and animals and as much of the variation in cultivated plants and domesticated animals as possible, diversity is rapidly disappearing all over the world. In 1991, the Rural Advancement Foundation International (RAFI) estimated that the world's twenty major food crops had already lost 70 percent of their previous diversity due to human activities. The remaining diversity continues to disappear at an estimated rate of 2 percent per year for those vital twenty crops. Just three of them—corn, wheat, and rice—account for half of the calories consumed in the world every day. Yet these three crops have been becoming less diverse at an especially alarming rate: Japan has lost two-thirds of its rice varieties since the turn of the century; just six varieties of corn make up 71 percent of the U.S. harvest; and modern wheat varieties have pushed out locally adapted natives in the very areas where wheat originated, such as Turkey. Why is this happening?

Breeding for High Yield

As the world has shrunk and human populations have exploded, the focus of plant and animal breeders has been on producing plant varieties with the highest yield and on developing animals that produce the most meat, milk, or eggs. In addition, the movement of human populations away from rural areas, where they could grow their own

---

Previous page: Just a sampling of heirloom potato varieties, each with its name. Notice the variations in size, shape, skin texture, and shade; the colors range from near white to dark purple. PHOTO BY DAVID CAVAGNARO

food, into cities, where they must rely on others to feed them, has resulted in larger farms that produce crops and animal foods for sale rather than primarily to feed the farm family. These powerful trends have overwhelmed the kinds of local crop varieties and animal breeds that once fed the populace all over the world. The scientific understanding of heredity has spurred efforts at plant and animal breeding to meet goals such as high productivity or uniform harvest rather than preservation of diversity. "Improved" varieties of crop plants and animal breeds have spread around the world, pushing out the older, locally adapted types, called land races. And the ever-increasing pressure on the land by the growing human population of the planet has resulted in the destruction of an alarming amount of the habitat where wild relatives of crop plants and domesticated animals once lived.

The Varied, Imperiled Potato

Potatoes illustrate some of the problems in preserving diversity. They have become one of the most important crops in the world, in large part because the wild potatoes and cultivated land races gathered by plant collectors have provided vital genes that helped the potato adapt to a variety of growing conditions. Genes from wild potato species have also improved crop yield, increased the starch content—and hence the "fluffiness"—of the tubers, and contributed to resistance to many diseases besides late blight. "Wild" genes, as well as those from land races, are looked to as sources of resistance to frost and to pests such as the Colorado potato beetle and nematode worms. Some potatoes grown in North America possess nutritional bonuses gained from using land races from South America. A variety called Butte, for example, has significantly in- creased protein and vitamin C content.

Potatoes are grown in more than 130 countries, and the world crop is worth more than $100 billion each year. Potatoes do well in northern areas where other crops may fail, and they yield almost twice as much per acre as do grains such as wheat. Today, the potato thrives at eleva- tions ranging from below sea level, in Dutch fields pro- tected by dikes, to nearly fourteen thousand feet in the Himalayas. Potatoes grow in climates ranging from that of the chilly Arctic Circle to hot, dry deserts.

The greatest variety of potatoes is found in the Peru- vian Andes, where the edible species evolved. Tubers in various shades of white, brown, red, and black come in an amazing array of shapes and sizes, from tiny berry-size nuggets to giant long, bumpy cylinders weighing several pounds. Altogether, eight species of potato can be grown for their nutritious tubers. More than sixty wild relatives will also cross easily with potatoes, providing an especially varied gene pool to work with.

The Quechua language of Peru has at least a thousand words for potatoes, and Andean farmers grow between 3,000 and 5,000 varieties. But despite the number of existing potato species and varieties, the diversity of com- monly cultivated types grown outside Latin America is surprisingly limited. In the United States and Canada, a mere six varieties, all from the same species, comprise 80 percent of commercial potato production.

In the United States, just one variety—Russet Burbank—makes up 60 percent of the harvest. Why? McDonald's chose this variety as the only one for its famous french fries. With McDonald's expanding operations around the world, its increasing demand for Russet Burbank may lead local potato farmers to decide to plant that variety rather than others.

Saving Potato Variability

Some scientists are doing their best to save the precious genetic variability of the potato. The World Potato Collection in Peru preserves more than thirteen thousand different strains. The collection is a project of the International Potato Center in Lima. Here, in addition to guarding the genetic variability of potatoes, researchers strive to develop improvements in commercial potatoes that will make them easier to grow. They work to incorporate pest and disease resistance found in South American native potatoes into commercial varieties. One major project that paid off after twenty years of research is introducing a gene for hairy leaves, derived from a wild potato species, into commercial potato varieties. Hair on leaves may not sound important, but the hairs deter a variety of insect pests, reducing the need for pesticides. When touched by an insect, the hairs release a clear liquid that blackens and hardens on contact with oxygen, trapping the insects so they starve to death.

The workers at the International Potato Center are also trying to develop potatoes that will grow "true to seed"—when the seeds are planted, all the resulting plants will be much the same, producing potatoes that yield a

33

harvest at the same time and that are of the same type. Potatoes don't rely exclusively on their seeds for reproduction—they can also come back year after year from their tubers if they aren't harvested for food. Over the winter, the tubers remain dormant in the ground. In the spring, sprouts from the eyes (the dents you can see in the potato skin) form new roots and shoots. Wild potatoes and some of the domesticated ones grown in South America also readily form flowers that produce seeds. But commercial potatoes grown in most of the world develop flowers that drop off without forming seed-bearing fruits. Farmers have no choice but to plant pieces of the bulky tubers, which must be carefully stored during the winter so they won't sprout before planting time. It takes about a ton of potato tubers to plant one acre, while less than two ounces of seeds would accomplish the same task. In addition, the tubers can carry diseases from one season to the next. For this reason, commercial growers buy specially grown tubers that are disease-free rather than saving some of their own crop for planting the next year. In some countries, the cost of importing disease-free tubers amounts to almost half of all the cost of growing potatoes. This expense slows down the expansion of commercial potato growing in developing countries.

True potato seed would also be a boon to gene banks such as the Vavilov Institute. In order to keep a potato strain going, the tubers must be planted each year and then harvested. This process requires land, labor, and money, and every time a crop is planted out, it can be lost to pests, diseases, or bad weather. The tubers also take up precious storage space and must be kept cool during the winter. Seeds, on the other hand, take up little space and can be kept for several years between renewal plantings.

The Vanishing Potato

Despite the efforts of scientists to save potato varieties and wild potato relatives, many of each have disappeared and can never be brought back to life. Logging, overgrazing, and human population growth have destroyed much of the habitat of wild species. Andean farmers are also replacing traditional land races with commercial types that have higher yields and can be sold for cash. For their own use, the Andean people still prefer traditional potatoes. They don't like eating the "improved" varieties, which they find watery and poor in taste. But cash is an important commodity in the modern world, so farmers living close to cities—where the people who prefer the blander potatoes live—devote a large portion of their land to the potatoes they can sell for cash. For themselves, they grow a selection of the more floury native potatoes that can provide variety in their diet. Despite the preference of farm families for native varieties, the experts at RAFI fear that the introduction of true potato seed into the Andean highlands—in some ways a major improvement—would hasten the disappearance of traditional varieties.

As a result of the need for cash, farmland in the lower valleys where the commercial potatoes grow well may be planted almost 90 percent in modern potato varieties, and many traditional land races once grown in such areas are disappearing. But as elevation increases, more and more land is devoted to varieties that have sustained the mountain people for thousands of years. At approximately ten thousand feet, about half the fields are planted in native potatoes, and above twelve thousand feet, almost 90 percent of the crop is traditional varieties. At that elevation, ordinary potatoes just can't survive. Frost is an almost nightly occurrence, and only especially hardy land races with dry, bitter tubers will grow.

Not all native farmers are maintaining traditional potato varieties. Dr. Carlos Ochoa of the International Potato Center, who has been keeping track of potato varieties for several decades, finds that traditional ones are disappearing fast in Mexico and Guatemala. In northern Peru, the changes that have occurred are also alarming. In the late 1950s, Ochoa collected forty-five varieties in two areas. By the early 1970s, they all had disappeared from farmers' fields. The situation is especially sad for Ochoa: In much of the area he checked out, an improved variety he developed—ironically named Renacimiento ("rebirth")— had replaced the old potatoes. A number of these had not been collected and preserved before they were replaced by Renacimiento, so they are now extinct. Potatoes are disappearing in other areas, too. Vavilov's potato collection from the island of Chiloé off the coast of Chile included about two hundred types. Only twenty years later, half as many were found still growing on the island, with fewer and fewer remaining as time goes by.

In recent years, the effort to preserve the rich potato heritage of Peru has faced a new threat. A rebel movement called the Shining Path has waged guerrilla warfare in Peru, including a 1988 attack on a busload of workers from the International Potato Center. A guard was killed. A year later, storage buildings at an Andean station where the World Potato Collection was kept were dynamited. Because of the guerrilla threat, seeds, tubers, and plantlets growing in test tubes have been sent to safer sites in Peru as well as in other countries.

PART 2

THE
DIMINISHING
HARVEST

PITFALLS OF MODERN CROP BREEDING

An acre of farmland today is spectacularly more productive than it was a hundred years ago, thanks to the techniques of modern crop breeding. But the changes in how agriculture is conducted around the world have not all been positive. In the process of solving some problems, new difficulties were created. Now we must find ways of dealing with the legacy of scientific breeding and farming methods.

Feeding the World's Billions

For centuries, biological factors helped control the growth of the world's human population. But starting in the late nineteenth century, tremendous medical advances—first vaccination against deadly illnesses, then powerful drugs that stopped killer diseases in their tracks—resulted in dramatically increased survival rates for human offspring. As a result, the human population began to grow at an alarming rate around the 1940s. Governments and human service organizations became increasingly concerned that population growth would outstrip the food supply by the 1980s.

Governments began to cooperate with private institutions such as the Rockefeller Foundation and the Ford Foundation to establish research centers such as the International Maize and Wheat Improvement Center in Mexico and the International Rice Research Institute in the Philippines. The goal was to develop new varieties of

---

Previous page: When one kind of crop—such as these grapes— is grown in monoculture over many acres, growers are likely to run into serious problems with pests and diseases. PHOTO BY DOROTHY H. PATENT

plants that would increase the yield from each acre of cultivated land, thus increasing the world's food supply fast enough to keep pace with population growth and thereby stave off hunger and starvation. The American botanist Norman Borlaug developed new strains of wheat that produced double to triple the yield of traditional varieties. Before long, other researchers had achieved similar improvements in the yield of corn and rice. The results of these efforts were so striking that in 1970 Borlaug received the Nobel Peace Prize for launching the Green Revolution.

The new "miracle crops" were introduced in some Asian countries in 1965. They were widely accepted and covered over 10 million hectares (24.71 million acres) by 1970. Before the Green Revolution, many of these countries had been importing grain to feed their people. It took only three years for Pakistan to become self-sufficient in wheat, and within five years, India could produce enough grain to feed its people. Other countries had similar results. By 1976, 27 percent of the world's rice acreage and 44 percent of its wheat acreage were devoted to "miracle" varieties.

The Green Revolution Legacy

The Green Revolution may have been a spectacular success in terms of increasing crop yields, but it failed in important ways no one had anticipated. It accelerated the disappearance of family farms around the world, plunging large numbers of the people it was meant to help into deep poverty and despair. It also helped bring about the critical loss of genetic variability by replacing locally adapted land races with new, higher-yielding varieties. It greatly increased the amount of pollution generated by agricultural activity around the world. And it changed forever the way people all over the world, not just in the less-developed countries, grow their crops.

Growing the new varieties required changes in farming methods. For one thing, yield was increased largely through developing dwarf plants that devoted less energy to producing stems, leaves, and roots and more to developing grain. In order to grow well and produce fat heads of heavy grain kernels, the miracle varieties need chemical fertilizers added to the soil. They also have to be well watered, requiring irrigation systems. These small plants have a difficult time competing with hardy weeds, and the fertilizers and irrigation also promote the growth of weeds. As a result, chemicals that kill weeds, called herbicides, must be used.

Installing irrigation and buying the chemical fertilizers and herbicides costs money. The farmers who could afford the investment necessary to meet the needs of the new varieties had no choice but to plant only them in order to recoup their investment. And soon they discovered an additional expense—when acre upon acre consists of just one or two varieties of a single crop, pests are difficult to control. Yet another type of chemical had to be added to the mix—pesticides to kill the insects.

Too Many Chemicals

The barrage of chemicals—fertilizers, herbicides, and pesticides—has had a number of unfortunate consequences, some quite unexpected. In Africa, the roofs of huts collapsed because the pesticides had killed off the wasps that preyed on the caterpillars that ate the fronds used to make the roofs. Without the wasps, the caterpillars were free to munch away, destroying the roofs. The pesticides not only kill beneficial insects but they also accumulate in the environment, causing a health hazard to rural populations.

Chemical fertilizers contain high concentrations of nitrogen, the element that helps plants grow fast. Nitrogen is highly soluble in water, and nitrogen from the Green Revolution fertilizers washes out of the fields into streams and lakes. There, it encourages the growth of algae just as thoroughly as it increases the harvests in the fields. Algae use up the oxygen in the water needed by fish, and the fish die. In the rice paddies, the chemicals kill the fish that grow there, depriving farm families of an important source of high-quality protein and extra income. The use of manufactured fertilizers instead of traditional manures and composts also results in a decrease in soil quality. Soils that are chemically fertilized lose the valuable organic humus layer, which helps retain moisture. Without humus to hold on to water, soil erosion increases. The soil dries out faster, topsoil can blow away, and once-productive farmland can turn to desert.

Leaving Out the Poor

Did the poor benefit from the Green Revolution? Its purpose, after all, was to feed the world's hungry people. Unfortunately, this purpose has not been fully realized.

In four Philippine villages that switched to growing modern rice varieties during the 1970s, yields went up 70 percent. But despite that increase, incomes fell by as much as 50 percent. Not only did the expense of buying pesticides, fertilizers, and herbicides cut into profits, the increased yield led to a drop in the price farmers could get for their harvest.

In many countries, the revolution left the poor behind. Even with fertilizers, the miracle varieties need fertile soil, which is more likely to be owned by wealthy farmers than by poor ones. The intensive, highly technical methods of farming favored owners of large plots who had Western educations. Poor farmers have neither money nor large enough tracts of land to make an investment in expensive equipment worthwhile, so small farmers could no longer compete in the marketplace. Many gave up farming as a result and migrated to the cities, swelling the ranks of the urban poor living in slums on the outskirts of big cities.

Thus, the problem of the rural poor has been transformed in many countries into the more difficult problem of the urban poor. These people are not now growing any food to feed their families, and they have little or no money to buy food. Although some countries that once imported food now have enough in theory to feed their populations, in fact, much of that food does not go to feed people. About one-half of all the wheat, corn, barley, oats, rye, and sorghum grown throughout the world goes to feed animals, not humans. In addition, some countries with hungry poor earn cash by exporting food needed at home.

Diversity Disappears

Green Revolution policies favored the loss of genetic diversity in a number of ways. In some countries, governments made an effort to help poor farmers. In the Philippines, for example, the government offered loans to poor rice farmers. In order to qualify, the farmers had to plant only varieties from the list of ten rices that the government sanctioned. But the islands encompass an immense range of environmental conditions—the difference in latitude from the southernmost to the northernmost islands in the Philippines is about the same as from Houston to Minneapolis—so a rich heritage of well-adapted, native varieties was being grown. Countless numbers of these have disappeared. All over the country, the requirement of planting the new varieties in order to get loans led farmers to discard the old, familiar rice varieties and throw in their lot with modern times, even though the required varieties were more difficult to grow in many areas.

During the 1970s, Greek law required its farmers to plant only wheat varieties developed by the international institutes. Within a few years, the native land races, with their precious diversity, disappeared in all but the most remote mountain areas.

America Joins the Revolution

The philosophy of the Green Revolution—grow more grain on less land—has been enthusiastically adopted by American agriculture. The health of our farmlands has suffered as a result. Farm fertilizer use in the United States has increased tenfold since high-yielding corn varieties were introduced. Just as in other countries, runoff from farms is now a major cause of water pollution in the United States.

With the prevalence of monoculture—growing one crop on large plots of land—pesticides have become essential on the modern American farm, just as they have elsewhere. More than a hundred pesticides are used on apples alone. Yet the Environmental Protection Agency (EPA), a branch of the U.S. government, ranks pesticide residues on food as the third biggest cancer risk in the country. The two top risks—workplace chemicals and radon gas in homes—don't affect the general population the way pesticides in food do, and home owners can easily deal with high radon levels if they are found. Many scientists believe the EPA underestimates the health risk from pesticides. The EPA doesn't take into account the combined risks of exposure to more than one pesticide, even though we can be exposed to a number of different potentially dangerous chemicals at any given meal. Of the 600 chemicals used to make some 50,000 different deadly pesticide blends, only 125 have undergone tests to determine how much the body can tolerate. In addition, EPA figures for how much pesticide residue is allowed in foods are based on doses adults can tolerate. Children, because of their smaller size, fast growth, and life expectancy, are much more vulnerable to the effects of pesticides in food.

Chemicals once thought to be safe and used in large quantities can have effects that don't show up until years later when it is too late to do anything but wish things had been done differently. In 1993, one scientific study found that women with breast cancer had four times the level of DDT in their tissues than that of healthy women. DDT was banned in the United States during the 1960s, but it persists in fatty parts of the body like the breasts. In addition, this powerful insecticide is still used in other parts of the world and may be getting into the American food supply through imported produce. The incidence of breast cancer has been on the rise for many years, with the medical community puzzling over the cause. If the increase is due to pesticides used decades ago, we can only brace ourselves for the results of our past folly and hope that the government requires more reliable tests of safety for chemicals in use now and in the future.

Breeding for Uniformity

How was it possible to develop the high-yielding varieties that have revolutionized agriculture worldwide? Scientists had the tools available—all they needed to do was to utilize them in a strongly focused way.

Professional plant breeders look at agriculture in a completely different way than do traditional farmers such as the Hopi and other Native Americans. Instead of reveling in the variations that the teamwork of nature and humankind has developed over hundreds of generations, modern plant breeders strive for as much uniformity as possible. Uniformity is a virtue because it means all the crop will mature at the same time, with plants the same height producing grain (or other crop) with predictable traits. The entire crop can be harvested at once by efficient machines.

But plants that are genetically uniform tend to have serious problems. When breeders strive for uniformity, they end up with weak plants that have to be babied to survive. Along with the genes for the traits they desire—high yield, quality produce, and so forth—come genes for undesirable traits such as weak roots or susceptibility to diseases. Remember that every plant gets one gene for each trait from the female parent and one from the male parent, and that genes come in a variety of forms, called alleles. For example, in a plant with one gene that determines flower color, there may be one allele that results in red flowers and another that produces white ones. The flower color genes induce their effects by controlling the manufacture of pigment in the flower. The red gene tells the cells in the flower to make a red pigment, while the white gene results in no pigment being manufactured, making the flowers white. If a plant gets two red alleles, one from each parent, the flowers will be red. A white allele from each parent will result in white flowers. If, however, it gets a red allele from one parent and a white one from the other, the flowers will be pink—there is only one allele directing the manufacture of red pigment, so only half as much is made as in a red flower.

With many traits, one allele is enough to bring about the full expression of a trait. In such cases, that allele is said to be dominant. If, for example, the gene controls manufacture of a vital chemical needed by cells, one allele directing production of that chemical may be all the cell needs to function normally. An allele that shows its effect only when it has been inherited from both parents is said to be recessive.

When breeders strive for uniformity, they keep selecting for plants that are as much the same as possible.

The more similar the plants are, the more of their genes have two identical alleles. If these alleles result in a defect of some sort, the plants are weak or may even not survive.

The Hybrid Solution

Breeders have a way to get around the apparent incompatibility between uniformity and vigor. They develop two separate lines, each of which is inbred to be as uniform as possible. Each of the two lines carries some desirable traits. One might produce an abundant early crop, while the other might have plants of the right size that are resistant to serious diseases. Each of these strains may grow weakly, requiring a great deal of special care to mature successfully. But then, when it comes time to produce seeds to sell to farmers, the breeder crosses the two strains with each other. The resulting seeds carry one copy of the allele from the male parent and one copy from the female for each gene. Since the two parental lines have been bred to be quite different, the offspring will have two different alleles for most genes, giving them a "hybrid vigor" that their inbred parents lacked.

Hybrids enabled the success of the Green Revolution and modern agriculture in general; most of the high-yield varieties grown today are hybrids. But hybrids have one big disadvantage for the farmer that is a boon to the breeder. Farmers can save seeds from nonhybrid varieties to plant the next year. Such "open-pollinated" varieties produce seeds that will result in plants similar to their parents. But saving seeds from their own fields will not work for farmers who grow hybrids. If hybrids are allowed to go to seed, the carefully chosen alleles will get all mixed

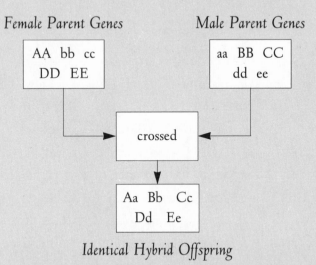

HOW HYBRID PLANT VARIETIES ARE CREATED

Female Parent Genes   *Male Parent Genes*

AA bb cc
DD EE

aa BB CC
dd ee

crossed

Aa Bb Cc
Dd Ee

Identical Hybrid Offspring

(Note: For simplicity, only four genes are shown in this diagram
and the next, indicated by letters of the alphabet. The capital letter stands
for one allele of the gene; the lowercase letter represents a different allele.)

Hybrid plant varieties are produced by developing highly inbred female and male parent strains. These strains may not grow and produce well themselves. However, when crossed with each other, they produce uniform hybrid offspring that combine the desirable traits of both parent strains.

up in the offspring. Some seeds will end up with two "good" alleles for a particular trait while others will have two "bad" alleles. Each species carries thousands of genes, and the alleles for each one are distributed at random in the offspring. Instead of being uniform like their parents, the plants in the next generation will vary greatly, and

WHY HYBRID PLANTS DON'T PRODUCE UNIFORM OFFSPRING

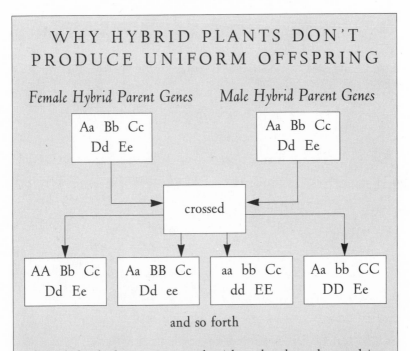

Female Hybrid Parent Genes   *Male Hybrid Parent Genes*

Aa Bb Cc
Dd Ee

Aa Bb Cc
Dd Ee

crossed

AA Bb Cc
Dd Ee

Aa BB Cc
Dd ee

aa bb Cc
dd EE

Aa bb CC
DD Ee

and so forth

If the hybrid plants are crossed with each other, the resulting offspring will show a mixture of traits derived from the parents. For example, the Aa alleles from the female parent and the Aa alleles from the male parent can combine to form AA, Aa, or aa configurations in the offspring. The same sort of recombination can occur for any of the thousands of genes the plant possesses, producing a great variety of unpredictable gene combinations in the resulting plants.

many could produce poorly or be extremely susceptible to diseases.

Thus, the farmer who wants a reliable crop from a hybrid variety cannot be self-sufficient and save seeds from his own fields. Not only does he have to have enough cash every year to buy fertilizer, pesticides, herbicides, and gas for his equipment, he must also have enough money to buy seeds. The companies that sell the seeds have a guaranteed market, since farmers who grow high-yielding hybrids must buy from them. Even when nonhybrid varieties are available, saving seeds won't help the farmer for long. In the modern, fast-changing agricultural world, a new crop variety lasts only about five years—after that length of time, it either succumbs to pests or diseases or is replaced by one with a higher yield.

Who Benefits from Modern Methods?

As a whole, the world today produces just enough food to feed its population—if it were properly distributed. Without modern, high-yielding varieties, there probably would not be enough food to go around. But we've already seen that this increase in food production comes at the price of degradation of the environment of all living things on the planet and that despite the amount of food produced, thousands of people still starve each year.

Modern farming methods produce more food, but they can be a burden for poor countries. Manufacturing fertilizers, herbicides, and pesticides; running the tractors and other equipment necessary to manage large fields; and pumping the water necessary for irrigation all take energy, which requires the use of oil and other natural resources. Poor countries can only afford to import so much oil and to devote so much of their limited energy resources to agriculture. Partly because of the need for cash to buy oil and agricultural chemicals, many poor nations now carry huge international debts, making it even harder for them to compete in the world economy. Cash-poor countries that could once count on their rural populations' ability to feed themselves are now plagued by large numbers of urban people who have no way of providing for their own needs. Some of these nations, such as Brazil, have tried to solve this problem by sending their dispossessed peasants into the rain forests to eke out a living from the poor rain forest soils after chopping down the trees. This process further speeds the loss of biodiversity on the planet, including the extinction of species related to crops and domesticated animals.

Ultimately, two groups benefit most from the switch to big farms that grow hybrid varieties requiring high chemical input: large farms and the producers of agricultural chemicals and seeds. Farmers with large landholdings, especially farms large enough to become mechanized and employ fewer workers, have experienced a doubling or tripling of the amount of grain produced from each unit of land. All over the world, agriculture continues to become more of a corporate business and less of a family affair. The biggest winners are the companies that produce the agricultural chemicals and provide the seeds. With millions of farmers beholden to them for necessary supplies, these companies have grown bigger and bigger and have expanded the range of what they produce, gaining ever more control over the world's food supply.

Traditional farming methods have favored the evolution of diversity in crop plants and domesticated animals. Over the thousands of years that people around the world have been raising plants and animals, an incredible number of varieties have been developed to meet human needs. Farms were small, and their main purpose was to raise food to feed the family. Producing excess to sell for cash was a secondary goal; survival of the family came first. Farmers saved seeds from their crops for planting the next year, and the wise ones kept only seeds from the plants that produced the best harvest. In that way, they developed varieties that could survive and yield a reliable harvest under the soil and climatic conditions of their farms. Over the generations in areas where people have lived for thousands of years, countless distinct local varieties of crops, called land

Up Close:
TRADITIONAL FARMING SYSTEMS

races, came about, each adapted to the conditions of climate and soil that prevailed in the area. The variations in land races are especially pronounced in mountainous areas, where populations in the valleys had little contact with one another and where growing conditions varied greatly with elevation.

A farmer's animals also had to be able to do well under local conditions, providing milk, eggs, and meat for the table, with perhaps a little left over for sale or barter. Domesticated animals had to tolerate extremes of climate —in some areas, both hot, humid summers and bitterly cold winters—often without the protection of a sheltering barn. They needed to be able to fight off infections, since there were no antibiotics to cure them. The animals often had to fend for themselves, foraging in nearby uncultivated land or in the barnyard and feeding on farm wastes such as crop resi-

In El Salvador, as in much of the Third World, many farmers still employ
traditional methods that require hard work but minimal use of chemicals.

PHOTO BY DAVID CAVAGNARO

dues and whey from cheese-making. Just as with plants, domesticated animals evolved into a great number of different breeds all over the world, each breed suited to its locale.

A traditional farm devoted to raising food to feed a family is a dynamic place. Land is used carefully to get the most that the soil has to offer, pro-mote soil fertility, and discourage pests and diseases. In a typical Native American garden, corn, beans, and squash share the same plot. Beans are planted next to each corn plant. The beans use the cornstalks as supports, climbing up them to reach the sun. In return, the roots of the bean plants take nitrogen from the

57

air pockets in the soil and combine it chemically in a way that makes it available to the demanding, fast-growing corn. Meanwhile, squash vines snake over the ground under the cornstalks, covering the soil and shading out weeds. This system works beautifully. All three dimensions of the garden plot are utilized. The plants help one another, and the farmer does not have to spend money on fertilizer or waste time weeding his plot. When time comes to eat the harvest, the three crops complement one another nutritionally, providing complete protein and a wide range of other important nutrients.

This sort of farming has additional benefits. When crops are grown in mixed fields, insect pests do minimal damage. One study showed that 60 percent of plant-eating insects were less abundant on mixed fields than on those with only one crop. Another experiment demonstrated that beans grown with corn had 45 percent fewer destructive leaf-eating beetles and 25 percent fewer leafhoppers than beans grown alone. The corn benefited as well, being bothered by 23 percent fewer army worms than was monocultured corn.

In Asia, traditional farmers use their rice paddies for maximum food production. Rice grows in shallow water. Not only does the paddy grow rice in its shallow water, it produces fish for the farmer's table. The fish consume weeds and eat mosquitoes that can carry human diseases, while their body wastes fertilize the rice. Rice paddies can yield a half ton of fish per hectare (2.471 acres—about 10,000 square yards). In addition, the water buffalo used to cultivate the paddies fertilize them with their manure and provide the family with milk and meat.

Traditional farms also tend to grow a mixture of varieties of a given crop. By planting more than one kind of bean each season, for example, the farmer can hedge his bets about growing conditions that year. Some of the plants will do better when there is lots of rain, while others may thrive under drier conditions. Cool weather will favor some types, while others do well in the searing heat. In this way the farmer is likely to get a crop unless the weather is really disastrous.

Different land races may do better on various plots of the farm. In rural Sierra Leone, Africa, farmers use a number of rice varieties to take advantage of climate and soil conditions. Rice that ripens early, providing the family with food before the main harvest, is planted low in the valley where the waterlogged soils retain water even in the dry season. The rice is harvested before the annual rains cause the valley's river to overflow its banks. Varieties that take longer to ripen but produce more abundantly are planted on the slopes, while the slowest maturing, flood-tolerant types are grown in the wetlands. In one village, forty-nine rice varieties are planted, each with its own special characteristics that are matched to specific growing conditions.

Growing a mixture of varieties is also advantageous nutritionally—the varieties can vary significantly in nutrient content. The lima bean varieties grown by the Hopi Indians, for example, are far from uniform. There is an eightfold variation in the sodium content, a 30 percent difference in protein, a threefold difference in iron. Some varieties contain four times the amount of fat as others. By eating a mixture of all these beans, the farm family receives some dietary variety even from the one food.

CHAPTER FIVE

WHO CONTROLS
AGRICULTURE?

Farmers traditionally tend to be independent, proud of their ability to produce food that feeds not only their own families but others as well. They have always lived by nature's timetable, not a man-made schedule that says to start work at 9:00 A.M. and quit at 5:00 P.M. five days a week. Farmers have always felt more in touch with the cycles of the natural world than most other people. But modern agricultural practices make farming more and more a scientifically scheduled business that depends on outside input and less and less an earth-centered art that encourages self-sufficiency.

The need for cash to buy seeds and supplies puts pressure on farmers to plant crops they can sell for cash rather than use for food to feed the farm family. Seventy percent of farming materials today come from the nonfarm sector and must be bought by the farmer. American farmers now spend almost two-thirds of the money they bring in to buy feed, seeds, fertilizer, pesticides, livestock, petroleum products for their equipment, and electricity.

Giants in Control

Before the 1970s, countless small, independent companies provided seeds to the world's farmers and gardeners. Their catalogs offered a tantalizing selection of varieties to choose from, often unique strains lovingly developed by family businesses and proudly offered to the public. All that has changed. When the companies that provided the chemi-

---

Mechanical harvesting is efficient, but the machinery is expensive, making it practical only for farmers with large landholdings kept in monoculture. PHOTO BY WILLIAM MUÑOZ

cals required by the Green Revolution began to realize they could make money selling seeds as well as chemicals, they began buying up seed companies. No one knows how many independent dealers have disappeared, but giant firms have taken control of almost a thousand since 1970. Now, instead of getting seeds from companies with names like Florida Seed and Feed or Asgrow Seed, the suppliers have names like Upjohn (known largely for its drugs) and Reichold Chemicals. Many of these corporations readily cross national boundaries. Suiker Unie, for example, owns nine seed houses in five countries.

It may seem strange that a drug company or one that makes chemical fertilizers would become involved in selling seeds. But more than a quarter of prescription drugs are derived from plants, so drug companies have always been familiar with botanical research. The connection for chemical companies is more direct—they can develop seeds that produce best when grown with their fertilizers, insecticides, and pesticides. Big millers that manufacture flour are also naturals for the seed-selling business—they can sell farmers the seeds, then buy the grain grown from those seeds.

Through the 1980s, such companies spent about a billion dollars each year buying up seed suppliers. Royal Dutch/Shell, the biggest pesticide manufacturer of all petroleum companies, is now also a giant among world seed companies. Of the world's top ten seed companies, only four sell seeds as their main business. Three of the others are primarily chemical firms, while one is a pharmaceutical giant. Food processing and trade are the major businesses of the other two. All but one—Takii of Japan —are headquartered in the United States or Western Europe.

Providing both seeds and chemicals opens up big op-portunities for profit and for control of agriculture. For example, in the early 1980s Ciba-Geigy sold sorghum seeds coated with a chemical that protected them from the herbicides Ciba-Geigy also sold. The herbicides controlled a wide range of weeds that might compete with the sor-ghum. But in order to use the herbicides to full advantage, the farmer had to buy the protectively coated seeds from the same company.

Many of these huge companies link their seeds with their chemicals. Thus, Stauffer Chemicals bought up three seed companies that dealt in corn seeds, and Stauffer offers herbicides and pesticides especially for corn. Upjohn is now both a breeder of field peas and soybeans and a pro-ducer of agrichemicals for beans.

When companies that sell chemicals as well as seeds are major developers of new seed varieties, serious prob-lems arise. The world's farmers should be using fewer agri-chemicals, not more. Pollution from chemicals is causing many problems for the environment and for human health. But the companies benefit most by producing seeds that require chemicals, not those that can do well without them. Also, when new varieties are developed only in the presence of pesticides, any pest resistances that might be present are masked. The only way to reduce dependence on chemicals is for varieties to be created by organizations that have nothing to do with the chemical industry.

The Struggles of the American Small Farmer

Over the last fifty years or so, American farmers have had a difficult time making a living. The federal government developed policies in the 1940s and 1950s that favored large farms. The policy was no accident—as Ezra Taft Benson, secretary of agriculture under Eisenhower, put it, "Get big or get out." Large farms could benefit most from price-support policies that paid farmers for certain key crops even if the prices dropped. When surpluses of grains were large, farmers were paid by the acre not to plant crops. If a farm was big enough, the farmer could make a living simply by *not* farming.

Between 1940 and 1967, twenty-five million Americans had to leave their farms. By 1990, the number of Americans living on farms had fallen from 23 percent of the population to less than 2 percent. The efficiency of mechanical harvesting favors large farms, since the equipment is prohibitively expensive for small farmers. Half of what we eat is now grown on only 4 percent of American farms, and a third of it comes from a handful of superfarms, many of which are owned by multinational corporations. Large farms that are mechanically harvested grow genetically uniform crops so that all the plants can be harvested at the same time.

The push for uniformity and for large farms comes from another direction as well. The increase in use of grains for processed products requires that the chemical composition of the seeds be predictable within a narrow range. Consider corn, for example. Tom Urban, chairman of Pioneer Hi-Bred International, Inc., the world's largest

seed company, predicts that 25 percent of the corn produced in the United States will be processed into consumer products by the year 2000. In order for a processor
to make a product such as corn syrup with a uniform
sugar concentration, the grain it buys has to have a consistent set of characteristics. Variability—that is, genetic
diversity—just won't do. A processor will buy only grain
that it knows comes from branded seeds with established
characteristics in order to have predictable raw material to
work with. This requirement for uniformity also favors
big farms at the expense of small ones. Buying a reliable
supply of grain from a few large farms is much easier and
less chancy than purchasing in small quantities from a large
number of small farms.

High Tech Takes Over

Many of the developments that will provide the consistent
traits demanded by modern technologies will come about
through new ways of manipulating genes. Until the 1980s,
breeders had to experiment with crossing different species
and varieties until they found combinations of traits that
resulted in a cultivar possessing the blend of traits they
desired. But genetic engineering offers powerful tools for
altering the genetic makeup of organisms one gene at a
time. For example, the biotechnology firm Calgene engineered a gene that interrupts tomato ripening. The tomato
ripens only to a certain point, then stops. Genetic engi-
neers added this gene to a tomato variety, dubbed the Flavr
Savr, so the fruits can be stored and shipped in a semiripe,
firm state with no concern that they will ripen further
and become soft and bruised. The gene allows the tomatoes

to stay on the vine an extra five days, theoretically giving them that much more time to develop a vine-ripened flavor. Calgene has invested about $95 million in the Flavr-Savr and hopes to capture the $5 billion fresh tomato market. If this new variety becomes popular with the public, it will replace other varieties, further limiting the genetic diversity of the tomatoes grown by American farmers.

Patenting Nature

The entry of genetic engineering into agriculture creates new legal dilemmas. Seed companies and biotechnology firms don't want to invest millions of dollars developing new varieties with unique traits, such as the Flavr-Savr tomato, only to have their product taken over by other producers. Once a new gene has been incorporated into a commercial variety, it will be passed on to the next generation of plants, just like any other gene. With hybrid varieties, breeders have control over the market—farmers must buy seeds from them, since seeds from hybrids don't produce plants exactly like their parents. But if just one or a few genes impart a valuable trait, such as delayed ripening, the plant breeder is helpless to control what happens once the new variety reaches market.

The world's legal systems are struggling with how to handle this problem. On the one hand, a company should be able to make a profit from a new development arising from its research. But then the questions start: Should a naturally occurring gene that is discovered be patentable? Or should patents be limited to bioengineered genes like the Flavr-Savr one? If a gene comes from a land race or wild species found in, say, Guatemala, should that country receive some financial benefit from the discovery? Should life forms be patentable at all, because they are created by nature, not by humans?

Until recently, plants and animals were excluded from patent protection. In the 1970s, the United States joined the Union for the Protection of New Varieties of Plants (UPOV), established originally in Europe. A special way for protecting plant breeders, called the Plant Breeders' Rights system (PBR), was the essential feature of the UPOV. PBR gives the breeder exclusive control over reproducing a variety for commercial purposes for a certain time period. Once the variety has been released, however, others can use it in their breeding programs, and farmers can save seeds for planting the next year. Thus, the original breeder has a monopoly over initial sales of the variety but doesn't control it beyond that point.

The companies that breed new plant (and animal) varieties now want more exclusive control over their products. Instead of PBR, they want the equivalent of industrial patents—the kind that cover new inventions— for their biological developments. Under PBR, only the specific plant variety is covered. But with a true patent, anything from an individual gene to a complete organism could be patented. The only requirement would be that the item be something new, that it involve an invention (a nonobvious step) of some kind, and that it be useful. Such vague terms create enormous gray areas in the whole business of plant patenting. Can a gene be "invented" by humans? Can it truly be "new," especially if it is discovered in nature rather than created in the laboratory? Nature is constantly "inventing" new genes and testing them through the process of natural selection. Who is to say that even a gene developed in a laboratory is truly "new"—the same gene could have been produced in nature over and over again without our knowledge.

Aside from such theoretical problems, the practical consequences of patenting life forms are alarming and can lead to restricting the genetic potential available in developing new varieties of plants or breeds of animals. If a gene were patented, the variety containing that gene could not be used by breeders other than the original one in producing new varieties without obtaining permission and, most likely, paying a fee. But ever since the first domesticated plants and animals were brought into the human fold, free use of all existing races, varieties, and breeds has been crucial to the development and improvement of our food sources.

Under industrial patent law, general characteristics as well as specific properties such as identifiable genes can also be patented. The results can be absurd, granting the rights to a whole area of crop improvement to one company. This has already begun to happen in the United States, which now awards patents on life forms. One company was granted a patent giving it a monopoly on breeding sunflower seeds with a high content of oleic acid, which effectively stopped other breeders from developing varieties with high oleic acid.

Meanwhile, another patent has been granted for the development of cereals, which can mean any grain such as wheat or corn, with a high content of the amino acid tryptophan. The protein quality of grains with more tryptophan would be much higher than in current varieties, making such research vitally important in improving the diet of people worldwide. But this new patent could prohibit any breeder other than the patent holder from working on high-tryptophan grains of any sort. The U.S. Board of Patent Appeals decided in 1987 that animals as well as plants could be patented, opening up the same kinds of questions for the animal-breeding industry.

An Ancient Right Denied?

Since thousands of years ago when the first grain seeds were gathered and saved for planting the next year, farmers around the world have carefully set aside seeds from their harvest for the following year's crop. They chose only seeds from the best plants, those with the highest quality product, hoping that each year their harvest would be better than the last. In this way, the myriad land races of crop plants developed through the centuries, honed by the combined influences of nature and humankind. For farmers, saving seed is a vital part of their way of life.

But in the United States and around the world today, the right of farmers to control their genetic resources is being challenged by multinational seed suppliers. Under the American version of Plant Breeders' Rights, breeders have a limited monopoly over the production and sale of varieties they develop for eighteen years. The limits involve the rights of other breeders to experiment using one another's varieties (the breeders' exemption) and the right of farmers to save seed from their harvest to plant the next year (the farmers' exemption). The farmers' exemption also allows farmers to sell leftover seed they don't plant to other farmers. The American Seed Trade Association is trying to amend the breeders' rights laws to keep farmers from selling leftover seed. It believes only breeders should have the right to sell seeds of the varieties they develop. The association is also unhappy that farmers save seed for themselves, for this practice cuts into the market.

If farmers are forbidden to save seed and plant it, they will be completely beholden to seed companies, which would have a virtual stranglehold on the country's food supply. Not only would farmers lose their last shred of independence, the process of refining plant varieties to suit different environments would stop. Farmers would not be able to encourage the traits they prefer in the crops they grow. The evolution of genetic variability on American farms would cease, since every year all farmers would be forced to buy and plant the varieties made available by seed suppliers. Cornell University professor William Lesser calculates that prohibiting farmers from saving seed from just three crops—soybeans, wheat, and cotton—would cost American farmers more than $500 million a year. If the legal concept of forbidding seed saving were to spread around the world, small farmers in developing countries who couldn't afford to buy seeds would be forced out of business, leaving agriculture worldwide in the hands of giant corporations and causing the loss of the untold genetic diversity now encouraged by local growers.

Breeders and biotechnology companies claim they need strong legal protection for their products or developing new varieties won't be worth the investment. They hold out the promise of pest and disease resistance, which would drastically reduce the quantity of polluting pesticides farmers would have to apply to their crops. But instead, biotechnological research is going in a completely different direction, toward developing crop varieties that are resistant to herbicides.

According to a 1990 report by the Biotechnology Working Group, breeders are working on modifying at least thirty species of forest trees and agricultural crop plant species so they can withstand otherwise harmful doses of herbicides. More than thirty companies in the world are conducting research into herbicide-tolerant plants. Over 50 percent of genetically engineered varieties being tested in 1994 have been developed for herbicide tolerance. By concentrating on developing herbicide tolerance rather than pest resistance, companies can sell both their tolerant varieties and their herbicides to farmers. Farmers benefit by not having to plow up weeds in their fields. Spraying herbicides is quicker and more thorough than weeding, especially on giant farms devoted to monoculture.

Maintaining a balance in agricultural business is vital to the health of the world's economy and the planet as a whole. Companies that develop seeds and other products need the opportunity to profit from their research. But governments must protect the rights of the individual farmer as well as those of the seed companies.

PART 3

DECLINING
ANIMAL
DIVERSITY

CHAPTER SIX

MORE THAN
NOAH'S ARK

John Bender stops hammering on a new fence long enough to explain how he got into the business of raising rare breeds of livestock. "I got started with the Barbados blackbelly sheep," he explains, "And look where I am now." Bender's Mokelumne River Ranch near Stockton, California, is home to seven kinds of sheep, six breeds of goat, eight types of pigs, one unusual breed of cattle, and a large variety of barnyard birds.

Bender's goal is to help preserve endangered and ancient breeds of livestock, thus salvaging some of the genetic diversity of domesticated animals that is rapidly disappearing. While the potential usefulness of some breeds is presently not known, others have traits that show promise or have already proved their value.

Varieties of Sheep

The Barbados blackbelly sheep that got Bender started is a striking animal. This breed was developed about 350 years ago on the Caribbean island of Barbados from crosses between short-haired African sheep and woolly European breeds. A heavy coat of wool is fine in a cool climate, but not in the tropics, so the sheep were selected for a short coat of hair rather than wool. The black of their bellies extends down the insides of their legs, around the backs of their thighs, and marks their faces with a stripe next to each eye. The rest of the coat is a rich tan color. The sheep's wild and exotic appearance has led to its popular-

---

Previous page: Galloway cattle are popular with people who want a breed that is gentle on the land and requires little care. PHOTO COURTESY OF DEREK PRUITT, LAZER GALLOWAYS

ity on Texas game farms, where hunters pay a fee to shoot animals living in large enclosures.

The Barbados blackbelly's short hair and its flashy colors make it look very different from the more familiar sheep raised for their wool. But this gentle, intelligent breed has valuable traits. For instance, it is resistant to parasites and diseases. It is also prolific, producing twins or triplets twice a year and needing no special attention from the farmer. Barbados lambs are lean, providing the kind of meat desired by consumers who are concerned about dietary cholesterol and fat.

In a large pen on Bender's ranch are some small sheep whose long coats have mixtures of brown, black, gray, and white wool. One of the rams has four horns instead of the more familiar two. "These are Navajo-Churros, the oldest breed of sheep developed in the New World. They came from the Churro sheep brought over by the Spanish conquistadores in the sixteenth century. The U.S. government tried to get rid of them in the thirties and forties, but luckily it didn't succeed," says Bender.

Over the four hundred years since they came to America, the Navajo sheep have become a vital part of Navajo culture. Through natural selection in the harsh desert, they developed an ability to survive where other animals perished. Their special wool has long, coarse, outside guard hairs with soft, short wool underneath. It is perfect for making durable rugs and clothing.

The loss of their sheep due to government stock-reduction programs devastated the Navajos. After taking away the desert-adapted Navajo-Churro sheep, the government tried to replace them with "improved" breeds that couldn't survive in the harsh desert conditions. By the 1970s, only a few purebred Navajo sheep remained. The breed might have disappeared completely, taking with it the traits that enabled the sheep to survive in the hot, dry desert, but in the late 1970s, Utah State University professor Lyle McNeal took an interest in Navajo sheep and helped rescue the breed. Navajo sheep have returned to the reservation, and by 1988, more than four hundred of them were again living on the reservation, and many others were in private herds such as that of John Bender.

The Navajo sheep provide an important lesson. Just like land races of plants, animal breeds that have survived in a particular area for a long period of time have adapted well to the conditions prevailing there. The breeds brought in to replace the Navajo—sheep adapted to cool climates—may have had finer wool and thicker coats, but that same fine wool collected and retained sand. The coat's thickness also made the sheep ill-suited for the fierce desert heat—their bodies were so well insulated that they couldn't properly regulate their body temperature when they became too warm. For such sheep, having a thick coat in the desert was like a person being forced to wear a full-length fur coat at the height of summer.

Pigs and More Pigs

Bender points out two small, hairless black hogs in another pen, wandering among a bunch of Nubian and pygmy goats. "See those two? They're Yucatan miniature pigs from Mexico. Down there, people aren't concerned with preserving different breeds. But luckily this one didn't disappear. Now it's raised for medical research. Its body organs are about the same size and proportion as those of humans. The heart valves used to replace those in human hearts come from that kind of pig."

Yucatan miniatures were imported into the United States in 1960. Since then, some have been selectively bred from their original weight of about 160 pounds (75 kg) down to between 65 and 110 pounds (30 to 50 kg). This smaller variety of Yucatan miniature is called the Yucatan Micropig®. In the process of downsizing, the pigs have lost none of their vigor, intelligence, or gentleness. In addition to their use in medicine, these pigs make excellent stock for small farms, especially in hot, arid regions.

Another pig strolls by. She is a giant compared to the Yucatan miniatures. Her white-coated body is marked here and there by black blotches. Her gigantic ears flop over above her eyes—how can she see? Her eyes are downcast as she snuffles noisily about, foraging for bits of grain or other food missed by her companions.

"That's a Gloucester Old Spot," remarks Bender. "Look at her face—she always appears to be smiling." But the busy pig is already heading away, continuing her constant search for more to eat. The Gloucester Old Spot was developed as an independent, foraging animal that fed on whey left over from cheese-making and on windfall fruit in apple orchards. Such a breed was handy in the old days; the animals took care of themselves and fed on waste materials, then were slaughtered to provide valuable lard and meat. Today, the breed might be useful in developing commercial pigs that could be raised outdoors. But few farms keep pigs anymore, and only a couple dozen Gloucester Old Spots are found in North America. Even in Britain, where the breed originated, there were fewer than three hundred breeding sows in 1988.

North America has produced valuable breeds of pig, too. The Ossabaw Island hog evolved by natural selection, like a wild species, for more than four hundred years. In the 1540s, Spanish explorers released pigs on islands off the coast of Georgia, where they had to fend for themselves. Over time, these pigs developed some interesting and unusual characteristics. Like many island animals, they became smaller. They evolved a unique biochemical adaptation to the food availability on the island, where food is scarce in the early springtime. The Ossabaw Island hog can store fat rapidly when food is abundant and utilize it just as fast when food is scarce. It can store more fat on its body than any other mammal that lives in the wild. Its adaptations to a feast-or-famine lifestyle include a mild form of diabetes. Scientists have made important discoveries relating to both animal science and human health through studying this unusual natural trait.

In addition to its medical uses, this hardy breed can be valuable for subsistence farmers who want to raise pigs but don't want to invest much into taking care of them.

Farmers who have limited space might do better raising small pig breeds rather than large animals like the Ossabaw Island hog, which can reach 250 pounds in captivity. Breeds that get no larger than about 150 pounds are easier to raise on small farms. Small pigs are especially useful in the tropics because their bodies can cool more readily than those of larger pigs.

One pig breed, the Mexican Cuino, can weigh as little as twenty-seven pounds when fully grown. Unfortunately, many small pig breeds have already become extinct, especially in Europe, and those in Latin America and Africa are threatened. Fortunately, China—the world's largest pig-raising country—has made efforts to preserve native pig breeds.

Unusual Cattle

In a large enclosure at the back of the farm, a few large cows with long golden brown hair and big, sweeping horns are lying down as they chew their cuds.

"These West Highlands are my only cattle," Bender says. "Cattle take up too much space when you're trying to keep as many different breeds as possible."

West Highlands, also called simply Highland cattle, look so different from other breeds that people may not realize they are the same species. A Kansas farmer who raises them says passersby think they are buffalo or yaks. But West Highlands are cattle all right, and especially interesting, useful, and hardy ones at that. They will eat a more varied diet than most other breeds, clearing away unwanted weeds and brush in addition to grazing on grasses. Their thick coats enable them to survive extreme weather conditions, and they are resistant to diseases. These efficient animals can convert feed from even a poor pasture into tasty, tender beef. Fortunately, the West Highland breed is not endangered.

Another valuable Scottish beef breed is the Galloway. These cattle have a double coat of winter hair that is shed for summer, so they tolerate both heat and cold well. Like West Highlands, Galloways eat weeds and brush as well as grass. For decades, no one was interested in Galloways outside of Scotland. Fortunately, the Scots kept raising them, even though they were not big moneymakers.

In recent years, Galloways have become popular, especially in Germany, for a number of reasons, including their small size, attractive appearance, and gentleness. But their most important trait is their minimal impact on the land. Most cattle clip grass closely and can harm the roots through overgrazing. But Galloways graze more like wild bison, nipping off the blades of grass without damaging the plants. This mode of feeding actually stimulates the plants to grow more vigorously and to produce more nutritious leaves. Scottish farmers take advantage of this characteristic and alternate grazing sheep, which clip grass very close to the roots, and Galloways in their pastures. After the cattle have "repaired" the pasture with their gentle grazing, sheep can be put out again.

In Germany, Galloways are used in a similar way by rural residents who have small plots of land where they keep ponies. Like sheep, the ponies can cause damage with their grazing, eventually killing the grass and turning the pasture into a bare plot of land. But by alternating ponies with Galloways, the land can be regenerated, and the landowner can have a bonus of delicious, tender beef for the dinner table. Because they require little care, Galloways are also a good choice for people who don't know much about farming. On their own, without the hormone treatments or grain feeding given to commercially raised cattle, they produce lean, high-quality beef.

Closer to home, the Texas longhorn is a part of the romantic history of the West. This hardy breed developed largely from Spanish cattle brought over in the sixteenth

and seventeenth centuries. The cattle were left wild on
the vast plains of Texas, where they evolved to survive
in harsh, dry conditions. During the nineteenth century,
longhorns were driven in huge herds northward to the
Midwest to feed the nation. But cattle breeds imported
from northern Europe were more efficient at producing
beef, so the longhorns were almost allowed to die out. In
1927, the government decided to try to save the breed,
selecting twenty-one animals from southern Texas and
northern Mexico to begin a herd in the Wichita Mountains Wildlife Refuge in Oklahoma. At the same time,
private citizens also began to value the longhorn.

At first, efforts at saving these dramatic animals were
spurred by nostalgia for the Wild West. But in recent
years, their hardiness and ability to thrive while feeding
on cactus, brush, and other low-quality foods has sparked
renewed interest in the practical value of keeping longhorns. Longhorn bulls are also used for breeding young
cows of other breeds—the resulting calves are small and
have long, slender bodies, making birthing easier for first-
time mothers that may not yet be fully grown.

The Importance of Minor Breeds

Each breed of livestock has its own unique set of traits,
just like every variety or land race of crop plant. Breeds
consciously developed by people were selected for traits
important to them, such as the thick winter coat and beneficial grazing method of Galloway cattle or the independent foraging of the Gloucester Old Spot pig. Breeds that
developed in a feral state, such as the Ossabaw Island hog
and the Texas longhorn, have become fine-tuned to their

environment over time and can thrive with little or no attention from humans, making them especially easy to raise. Feral breeds also tend to be especially resistant to the pests and diseases that prevail in the areas where they live, a trait that breeders can draw upon to produce healthier animals requiring fewer chemicals to raise.

Minor breeds can end up with unforeseen uses, too, such as the important medical applications of the Yucatan pig and the Ossabaw Island hog. As with plants, no one can know what circumstances may arise in the future that will make a seemingly useless trait important.

The desire for leaner meat on the table could lead to a search among uncommon breeds for naturally lean animals. While the conditions under which animals are raised have a major influence over how much fat the meat ultimately contains, breeds show differences, too. The Japanese raise cattle known for their especially tender, juicy beef, meaning meat that is high in fat. When the fat content of the same part of one muscle (the one that provides us with tenderloin steaks and filet mignon) was measured, Japanese black steer meat contained 17 percent fat, while meat from the shorthorn—a British-American breed—had 8.6 percent fat. Both longhorn and West Highland cattle produce lean beef, and their genes could prove useful in developing the leaner meat consumers favor today.

Sheep also show big differences in fat content depending on breed. Just among British breeds, differences can be significant. For example, lamb carcasses from Suffolk sheep in one study were 32.9 percent fat, while those of another popular breed, the Southdown, were 38.5 percent fat. Sheep from countries with less-intensive farming practices—where the animals are left more to their own devices—seem to be leaner. Nigerian dwarf sheep measured only 7.4 percent carcass fat. It isn't known, however, how much of the difference between this figure and those for British breeds is due to heredity and how much to environment. Still, a number of minor breeds such as the Karakul carry up to 19 percent of their carcass weight in their tails, and most of that is fat. Such breeds could well have much less body fat than those commonly raised for meat in Western countries and could be a source for genes that promote leaner, healthier meat.

Unusual breeds can be useful for another reason, too. Some types, such as the Jacob sheep and Tamworth hog, appear to be closer to early domesticated animals than other breeds. By studying such breeds, scientists can learn about the origins of domesticated animals. Jacob sheep, which have spotted coats, are thought to be similar to the spotted sheep pictured on tombs of ancient Egypt. While the breed disappeared in the region where it originated, it was brought to Palestine, then to North Africa, and on to Spain. When the British navy destroyed the Spanish Armada in 1588, some animals probably swam to shore, establishing the breed in Britain. Fortunately, dedicated breeders kept the herds pure. Like Jacob sheep, the Tamworth represents a relatively primitive, unmodified version of pigs when they were first domesticated. This breed is the original bacon-type hog, and, like other breeds that have not been intensively refined by people, it is hardy and vigorous.

Cattle have played an important part throughout human history in Europe and Asia. First they were prey, hunted for their abundant meat, tough leather, and useful horns that could be made into various tools. Then they were domesticated, becoming valuable for their labor and milk as well as for meat, leather, and horn. Cattle spread wherever people lived, becoming an integral part of life in Africa, Australia, and North and South America in addition to their places of origin in Europe and Asia.

The wild ancestor of cattle, called the aurochs, is extinct. Once found all across the Northern Hemisphere except in North America, the last aurochs was shot in Poland in 1627. We have a good idea of what the aurochs looked like, for its image is among the famous prehistoric drawings gracing the caves of Lascaux in France, and the ancient Romans, including Julius Caesar, wrote of it. Aurochs were huge animals. The bulls were more than six feet (two meters) tall at the shoulder and weighed over a ton. Domesticated cattle are considered to be the same species as the aurochs.

The variety of domesticated cattle is stunning. While some breeds are versatile, most kinds were developed for one of two purposes: milk production or meat. Dairy cattle make copious quantities of milk, while beef breeds put on plenty of muscle. Within both types is tremendous variety. Cattle can also be divided up another way—the typical Western type, with erect ears and smooth skin, or the tropical zebu type, with drooping ears, a hump, and loose skin that forms a dewlap below the neck.

Cattle may have long horns, short horns, or no

Up Close: MANY VARIETIES OF CATTLE

*The gaur is a powerful, hardy relative of domesticated cattle
that might provide useful genes for crossbreeding.*

horns. All members of a breed, such as the Black Angus, may be the same color. A variety of striking color patterns can be valued, as in longhorns. The size of cattle also varies considerably. Bulls of beef breeds such as the Maine Anjou or Chianina can exceed two tons, whereas a fully mature dwarf West African shorthorn weighs in at no more than 340 pounds (150 kg).

In a few parts of the world, cattle are raised for other traits besides meat, milk, and draft power. Powerful black fighting bulls that challenge matadors are bred in Spain, while cows with fighting instincts are the specialty of Eringer cattle raised in part of Switzerland. A dozen or so cows go into the arena together and fight until one proves her superior strength. On the Indonesian island of Madura, cattle that are a cross between the wild banteng and domesticated cattle are bred for racing in yoked pairs pulling sleds. These Madura cattle are probably the fastest bovines in the world; one running free can gallop almost as fast as a horse.

The predominance of particular cattle breeds depends on what uses are important at a particular time and place. During the nineteenth century, the English longhorn was the most common cattle breed in Britain. Cattle then were valued for their working ability and for the amount of fat on their bodies, which was used as tallow for candle making. Then horses became more important as draft animals, and electricity began to take over the business of lighting buildings. By the turn of the century, meat and milk production had become the most important cattle traits. The versatile shorthorn, valua-

ble both for milk and meat, replaced the longhorn as the most popular breed. The rise of intensive agriculture in the middle of the twentieth century brought further changes. The Holstein-Friesian, a specialized dairy breed, became the prime milk producer, while bulls of big breeds from the European continent, such as the Charolais, were used to boost the size of British beef cattle.

Because of their versatility, cattle can be especially useful farm animals. The same cow can pull a plow, raise a calf, and provide milk for the family if she comes from a versatile, hardy breed.

Four wild relatives of domesticated cattle still live in Asia, and each may have something to offer as improvements. The banteng thrives in the tropics and is resistant to ticks and the diseases they carry. This beautiful animal lives in both wild and domesticated forms. The smaller, domesticated banteng is common in Indonesia and is especially valued in Bali. Wild banteng inhabit Indonesia and Indochina, but their populations are endangered because of the increase in the human population. Banteng will hybridize with cattle, and their ability to maintain health even on very poor pastures could prove invaluable to cattle ranching in marginal areas all over the world. They are also resistant to many diseases. Experiments are under way in Australia and Texas with banteng-cattle crosses.

Yaks are also both wild and domesticated animals. Unlike the sleek-haired tropical banteng, the yak's long, thick coat is adapted to the harsh, frigid climate of the high Himalayas. While domesticated yaks still exist in healthy numbers, the wild type is endangered because of uncontrolled hunting and habitat loss and is now found only in remote highlands where even the domesticated yak can't survive. Yak-cattle crosses, called yakow, can live at lower altitudes than yak but still need a cool climate. While yaks and yakows don't do well in warm areas, they are the only bovines that can work and produce meat and milk at very high altitudes.

The magnificent gaur lives over a wide range in Asia, although some populations are threatened with extinction. This powerful animal has much to offer domesticated cattle if crossbreeding succeeds: resistance to some parasites, ability to thrive on low-quality food, and enormous strength. In areas where cattle are left to their own devices much of the year, the gaur's great protectiveness toward its young and its ability to defend itself against predators as powerful as tigers could be advantageous.

The kouprey, the most primitive of living cattle, was discovered by the Western world only in 1937. The kouprey lives in southeast Asia and suffered greatly during the Vietnam war. It is close to extinction. Researchers are especially eager to learn more about this rare creature, for it may be immune to rinderpest, an especially virulent disease of cattle. Studying the kouprey could also shed light on the evolution of animals in the cattle family.

CHAPTER SEVEN

MODERN FARMS,
FEWER BREEDS

The immense changes in farming practices during the twentieth century have affected domesticated animals in much the same way as they have crop plants. The trend away from hardy organisms that can survive without human intervention and that can produce by utilizing what nature provides is just as true for domesticated animals as for crop plants. Maximum productivity is the greatest value, even when it requires a massive input of high-protein feed and veterinary care.

Many animals raised today on large farms, especially pigs and poultry, never see the light of day, for they are raised in crowded, confined conditions. As farms have increased in size and become specialized, animals have been bred more intensively for particular characteristics, while other, more general qualities have been ignored. Traits like hardiness and ability to take care of themselves are superfluous, for the animals are scientifically fed and treated with antibiotics to inhibit infections. Rapid growth, good feed conversion (producing as much meat, milk, or eggs as possible from their food), uniformity, and tolerance of crowded conditions are the hallmarks of modern commercial livestock.

The result of this quest for efficiency, specialization, and uniformity is a dramatic decrease in the number of breeds commonly raised. Black-and-white Holstein cattle make up about 70 percent of American dairy herds, with only four other breeds comprising almost all the rest. Eighty percent of all registered beef cattle are from two

---

Turkeys today are raised in a way that is economically efficient but requires genetically uniform stock. PHOTO BY WILLIAM MUÑOZ

91

breeds—the reddish brown-and-white Hereford or the usually black (but sometimes red) Angus. Crosses between just these two breeds make up a high percentage of cattle raised for their meat. North America also once harbored more than a thousand genetically distinct breeds, strains, and recognizable bloodlines of chickens. Fewer than fifty are left today.

The reasons for the alarming disappearance in animal diversity are basically the same as for crop plants. Where once every family farm had a few laying hens, a milk cow, a couple of workhorses, and a pig or two, corporate farms today have either no animals at all, because they raise crops, or hundreds to thousands of animals of one kind. The animals are likely to be all the same breed or type of crossbreed and may be closely related to one another.

Each type of animal has become extremely special-ized—beef cattle produce just enough milk to nourish their calves, while dairy cows channel their energy into making milk. Broiler chickens lay few eggs, while the bod-ies of egg-layers put everything into producing more and more eggs. Many farm animals have little chance of sur-viving unless they are carefully tended by people, who feed and shelter them and protect them from pests and diseases.

Just as many vegetables raised today are hybrids, so it is with animals—much of the stock raised commercially consists of crossbred animals, mixtures of at least two breeds. There are about three hundred breeds and local varieties of pigs in the world. Yet crosses among just eight pig breeds account for 90 percent of pork production in the United States, and two of these eight are becoming rare in their pure form; just two varieties make up 60 percent of the hogs raised today. Chickens, too—both egg-layers and those raised for meat—are largely crosses limited to a few breeds.

The Poultry Business

Raising poultry has become big business dominated by just a handful of companies throughout the world that function as "primary breeders." Like seed companies, most of these are subsidiaries of huge multinational corporations. Six corporations control egg-laying chickens, nine dominate the broiler chicken business, and only three provide the world with turkeys. Along with a few others that breed ducks and geese, these companies produce *all* the birds for the entire world's industrial market. The genetic resources of much of the world's poultry lie with these corporations. If one of them decides to drop particular breeding lines or get out of the business, those resources may well be lost to the world.

By breeding for maximum production, such companies rely more and more on a narrow genetic base, selecting intensively for traits that increase productivity. The process has been very successful economically. Egg production, for example, has increased spectacularly. In 1955, the average hen laid 192 eggs annually. By 1985, that number had increased to 247, with some hens laying more than 300 eggs in one year.

But such success came at a price in terms of genetic diversity and adaptability. The normal behavior for a chicken is to choose a nest and lay a limited number of eggs in the springtime when days begin to lengthen. The hen sits on the eggs until they hatch and tends her chicks until they are old enough to take care of themselves. In the old days, if a farm family wanted eggs to eat, they collected eggs from the henhouse each morning, risking pecks from the protective hens. By gathering the eggs instead of letting the hens brood, farmers got their chickens to continue laying for many weeks. But egg-laying didn't continue all year. In fall, the birds stopped laying eggs, molted their old feathers and grew new ones, then rested during the winter before beginning the cycle over again the next spring.

Gone are the days in America when most chickens lived this way, looking after themselves, feeding on pests in the garden and leftover grain, laying eggs for the family, and ending up in the stewpot when their egg production dropped off. The all-purpose barnyard chicken is becoming an agricultural dinosaur. Some family farms still keep a few laying hens. But today, the vast majority of chickens are destined either to be broilers that grow fast and are slaughtered at the tender age of a few weeks, or egg-layers that devote their lives to producing eggs for the table.

Egg-laying chickens are crammed into small cages. The sharp tips of their beaks are snipped off so they won't peck one another to death in their unnaturally cramped quarters. The chickens' only role is to lay eggs—as many as possible. Their production lasts only a few months. When the hens can no longer produce, they are discarded by the thousands, their bodies added to landfills because they cannot legally be used for meat.

Life for a commercial egg-layer is completely different from the natural pattern. Artificial lights fool the hens into continuously laying eggs with no break during the short days of winter. The desire to brood the eggs has been bred out of them, so they just keep laying, never experiencing the "broody" behavior that can also interrupt egg-laying. Their eggs roll away into a common trough, day after day after day.

In order to achieve these results, the genetic base of the world's chickens has become perilously narrow. All the laying hens in commercial egg farms come from crosses among three or four chicken breeds. Just one breed, the White Leghorn, dominates. That means that all over the world, the vast majority of laying hens share a significant number of genes, which could make them susceptible to a particular disease. With so little genetic diversity, they would not be able to adapt to changing conditions without the infusion of genetic material from the outside.

The chickens we eat have suffered a similar fate. Broiler chickens are bred to put all their energy into building meat as fast as possible. Unlike old-fashioned barnyard chickens, these birds do not walk around checking out the world, even if they have room to do so. They just sit in one spot, not wasting energy on moving about. The business of raising broilers commercially began in the 1920s in New Hampshire. Since then, it has become a national industry. Breeding chickens purely for meat production and feeding them special foods has had phenomenal effects on productivity. Since 1940, broilers have been bred that can be sold at half the age but twice the weight. They only need half as much food as before. In seven to ten weeks, broiler chickens can be brought from egg to market. As a result, chicken has gone from being the symbol of prosperity for politicians, who pledged "a chicken in every pot," to an inexpensive food that most Americans can afford to eat often.

But just as with egg-layers, the result of this intensive effort has been a drastic reduction in genetic variation. Most broilers are the product of crosses of birds derived from only two breeds, the White Plymouth Rock and the Cornish. All the birds have white feathers, which makes the carcass appear cleaner after slaughter. They are completely unable to care for themselves because their foraging instincts have been suppressed in favor of genes that prompt them to sit still and not "waste" energy.

Neither modern egg-layers nor broilers can make it on their own. They are lost if left to their own devices in the barnyard. When the Rodale Research Center in Pennsylvania, an organization concerned with organic farming, wanted to find a natural way to control weevils in an orchard, they decided to try chickens and bought commercially available stock. The chickens didn't know what to do outdoors; they had to be shut out of their shelter to keep them from huddling together inside. Finally, the Rodale people consulted experts on rare breeds and ended up trying Dominique chickens, a breed known for its intelligence and self-sufficiency. Instead of huddling fearfully together, the Dominiques roam around, foraging for food over a large area.

The Ultimate Artificial Animal

The turkey could stand as a symbol of the success of modern animal breeding programs and what they can accomplish. But it is just as much a symbol of what is wrong with present-day animal breeding practices.

When Europeans "discovered" North America, turkeys were the only native domesticated animals being raised on the continent. Indians in the American Southwest and Aztecs in Mexico both raised turkeys. Spanish explorers took the impressive birds back to Europe with them, where they quickly became popular.

Wild turkeys are beautiful, intelligent birds that can scramble nimbly through the brush and flap up into the trees for protection from predators. They can fly at a speed of fifty miles per hour and run at twenty-five. Their beautiful, lustrous feathers gleam with a metallic sheen in the sunlight. The hens are so wary and protective of their chicks that they are rarely seen by people. At the slightest disturbance, they melt into the underbrush, where their mottled brown feathers make them disappear in the shadows.

Domesticated turkeys in Mexico and Central America live freely, foraging around villages and farms for insects, berries, greens, seeds, and fruits. They require very little care and need almost no food to supplement their diet, but they are there to provide delicious meat for a special wedding or birthday feast. Their colors vary from white through mottled shades of gray or brown all the way to black.

Industrially raised American turkeys, however, are completely different creatures. They have plain white feathers. (Even if bits of feather remain on the carcasses, they are too light to notice.) Their chicks must be carefully coddled for the first few weeks as they succumb to disease or cool temperatures very easily. They even need to be kept indoors at the hint of bad weather because they don't know enough to come in out of the rain and can become chilled and die if they get wet.

As they mature, the turkeys become better survivors. But they can barely fly, perhaps making it to the henhouse roof (if they are allowed outdoors at all) before their bodies become so laden with meat that they can't get off the ground. When they are ready for slaughter, they can just waddle along, thrown off balance by the huge load of meat that has grown on their breasts. If a family that buys a turkey to raise for Thanksgiving decides to keep it rather than make it a meal, the poor bird's legs are likely to become bowed under the burden of its heavy breast, and it will lose its ability even to walk.

These pathetic creatures are the ultimate in modern animal breeding. They can't survive without plenty of attention from humans; they have been bred purely for their ability to put on lots of meat and to put it on *fast*. Just like most crop plants today, turkeys are scientifically bred hybrids. One line of birds is bred to produce the female parents of the birds sold for meat and another line is bred to produce the male parents. One reason for this specialization of male and female parent lines is that the characteristics necessary for a breeding hen conflict with those desirable for the dinner-table variety. If a breeding hen is going to lay a lot of eggs, she needs space inside her body for them to develop. But a turkey for the table needs a large breast that takes up space on the body, crowding out the insides. For this reason, the female parent line of tur-

keys has been bred to produce hens with large abdomens
to make space for egg production, while the male parent
line provides the genes for the meaty bird favored by the
consumer. The huge breasts of the males make them in-
capable of mating naturally, so turkey breeders must artificially inseminate the hens, taking sperm from the males
and introducing it into the reproductive tracts of the females. Without the help of humans, these overbred birds
couldn't even mate to reproduce their own kind.

When these two strains are crossed, the resulting birds
all have the desirable big breast. None of them are destined
to be breeders, only meat providers, so the small body
cavity doesn't matter. As long as they are carefully tended
by humans and protected from disease, these unnatural
creatures will grow quickly to slaughter size—commercial
turkeys can reach twenty pounds in as many weeks from
hatching.

The companies that control the genes of commercial
turkeys maximize the size of the birds and their efficiency
in converting grain into meat in order to maximize profit.
They have been spectacularly successful in reaching their
objectives, turning the turkey from a once- or twice-a-year
treat into a part of the everyday American diet. But the
long-term price, many feel, is too high. A company such
as Nicholas Turkey Breeding Farm in Sonoma, California,
one of the three major breeders in the world, does keep
more than two dozen strains of turkey in reserve as future
genetic resources. But those strains represent only a small
fraction of turkey genetic variability and are probably
closely related genetically. Since these stocks are treated as

carefully guarded corporate secrets, just like a recipe for a highly popular spaghetti sauce or a best-selling soft drink, no outsider actually knows what they are like. If the company can see no practical commercial potential for a particular strain, the company will eliminate it, wiping out whatever unique genes it may possess. The intense competition in the food-production business makes it uneconomical for the company to do otherwise.

As it is, the American domesticated turkey in general doesn't possess much diversity. The handful of turkey breeds outside Mexico and Central America today are almost exclusively descended from the birds taken to Spain in the sixteenth century by Spanish explorers. In the seventeenth century, descendants of these few birds were brought back to North America by settlers. They apparently interbred with wild turkeys in the eastern part of what is now the United States, producing a larger, heavier bird. Some of these were then reexported to Europe. Domesticated turkeys in Mexico and Central America are a reservoir of potentially useful genes, but these animals are disappearing in some areas. Unfortunately, the turkey that was domesticated independently by Indians in the Southwest is already extinct.

There are six types of wild turkey, which might be thought of as a source of different genes. But wild turkeys are notoriously difficult to keep in captivity; they will batter themselves to death against the wire of their cages. Introducing genes from wild birds into domesticated stock is a difficult business. For this reason, it is especially important to preserve what little diversity there is in our domesticated turkeys.

Trends for the Future

Unfortunately, the meat, milk, and egg industries are continuing to move in the direction of more specialization and hence toward less diversity rather than more. The animals that provide the products we consume are becoming increasingly dependent on their human keepers for survival and less able to take care of themselves. For now, the system is able to make money and to supply the American public with abundant and low-priced foods. But, as with crop production, raising highly inbred and specialized animals requires an intensive input of chemicals and energy. Most of the animals are routinely fed antibiotics. Not only do these chemicals help protect the animals from diseases under crowded conditions, they also increase their growth rate. Chickens, turkeys, and pigs are all raised indoors, necessitating a considerable input of energy to supply artificial lighting and heat. Beef cattle generally graze on pastureland until they are almost ready for slaughter, so they are able to take care of themselves quite well. But before they are slaughtered, the animals are usually penned together in feedlots, where machines dole out generous quantities of grain, the consumption of which puts weight on the carcasses and helps make the meat tender and juicy.

Beef cattle have yet to undergo the kind of specialized breeding that results in helpless animals that can't take care of themselves. But the push for uniformity is threatening diversity just the same. In 1988, for example, the beef industry hailed a scientific triumph that foreshadows greater uniformity and an alarming decrease in genetic diversity. Scientists successfully split a cow embryo, which ordinarily would have produced one calf, into seven pieces. Each piece was transplanted into the uterus of a different cow and subsequently developed into a healthy calf. Because the calves all resulted from the same embryo, they were identical. When individuals have exactly the same genes, they are said to be clones. The process of producing clones is called cloning. As in human identical twins, the calves' genes were all the same. If raised under the same conditions, such genetically identical calves will result in uniform animals that produce carcasses of the same size and quality. This is good news for the industry, for such predictable uniformity would enable factories to become more automated. Employing more machines and fewer people would save beef producers money over time. But the effects on the genetic diversity of our cattle could prove disastrous.

When breeders select for rapid growth, other important traits that could benefit farmers and ranchers can suffer. Animals that mature early have shorter productive lives. They also can require more input of food energy to produce the same amount of meat than animals that take longer to mature. Thus, the push for fast growth to market size can backfire, resulting in short-lived animals that use energy inefficiently and cost more to raise.

Animals and Biotechnology

Genetic engineering is the wave of the future for modern commercial animal breeding. Plant scientists are further along the path toward manipulating specific genes than are those who work with animals. But high-tech methods that are routinely in use promote increased productivity at the expense of genetic diversity, and others that are in the beginning stages of development or on the drawing board also encourage more uniformity.

Artificial insemination is a very useful tool in animal breeding. Semen taken from a male animal is introduced into the reproductive tract of the female. As we have seen, this method is now necessary to use in breeding turkeys for the table. But it comes in handy even for species that are perfectly capable of breeding on their own. Dairy cattle breeders are enthusiastic supporters of artificial insemination. Semen is taken from dairy bulls of genetic stock that produces large quantities of milk. The semen is frozen in liquid nitrogen and shipped all over the world. In this way, cows anywhere can be mated with these superbulls in hopes of increasing milk production in the next generation. Because of artificial insemination technology, just six families of Holstein cattle dominate dairy herds all over the world. Despite the large numbers of these cattle in existence, the genetic diversity they represent keeps decreasing.

So far, attempts to introduce single genes into farm animals have not been very successful. One such attempt was to increase the growth rate in pigs. Because the faster the animals mature, the sooner they can be slaughtered and turned into profits, breeders are always looking for ways to hasten animals' growth rate. A natural substance called growth hormone stimulates weight gain in animals. When researchers introduced extra growth hormone genes into pigs, the animals grew 18 percent faster and ate 15 percent less food. Their carcasses also had less fat. However, they suffered from a variety of diseases, including stomach ulcers, arthritis, and kidney disease. They died young and were unable to reproduce. In the future, scientists may discover a strain of hog that will tolerate the extra growth hormone better. If so, these animals would be in great demand, and the genetic diversity of our pigs would be further reduced.

All consumers who eat animal foods benefit from the uniformity and relatively low prices of the eggs, milk, and meat produced by modern factory farming. But for that low dollar price, we pay a high price in other ways. Not only is our society gambling with our future by ignoring the perils of reduced genetic diversity, it is also paying a price in damage to the environment, consumption of nat-ural resources, risk to health from chemical residues, and inhumane treatment of the very animals that feed us.

PART 4

PRESERVING DIVERSITY

CHAPTER EIGHT

BANKING
GENES

cientists have long realized that plants grown in other parts of the world can be used to improve Western crops. As early as the late nineteenth century, adventurous plant hunters who explored remote areas of the earth brought back samples of crop species as well as exotic wild plants. But even so, for many years, the Vavilov Institute in Russia was making the only organized effort to save and propagate land races and wild relatives of crop plants. In the 1940s, American scientists were alarmed to discover that only 5 to 10 percent of the 160,000 plant species and varieties collected from around the world and recorded since 1898 were still maintained in living collections. Something had to be done before what little was left was also lost. Four regional plant introduction stations were set up in Geneva, New York; Ames, Iowa; Experiment, Georgia; and Pullman, Washington. In addition, a special station just for potatoes was set up in Sturgeon Bay, Wisconsin. An American system for preserving diversity had begun.

As time went on, saving diversity became even more critical. Wild lands were being cleared to create homes and farmland to support the soaring human population. In the process, an unknown number of wild relatives of cultivated crops lost their habitat and became extinct along with countless other wild species. At the same time, the Green Revolution was accelerating the loss of land races of cultivated plants by replacing them with modern, high-yielding varieties. The combination of the replacement of

Previous page: Seeds for long-term storage in seed banks are kept in vats cooled by liquid nitrogen. PHOTO COURTESY OF USDA

land races with Green Revolution varieties and the loss of wild lands was deadly for crop plants and their wild relatives. During the 1960s, scientists sounded the alarm— land races and wild relatives of crop plants had to be collected and preserved quickly, or humanity would lose an irreplaceable resource.

At that time, a few of what are now called gene banks already existed, the best known being the Vavilov Institute. The United States government had also established the National Seed Storage Laboratory (NSSL) at Fort Collins, Colorado, in 1958. The goal of seed banks was and is to preserve as much of the variation in cultivated crops and their wild relatives as possible.

In the early 1970s, the United Nations and the Consultative Group on International Agricultural Research (a consortium of governments, private foundations, and lending agencies, abbreviated CGIAR) called for the establishment of international agricultural research centers and genetic resource centers, especially for the tropical and subtropical crops in developing countries. By 1985, a hundred countries had set up almost 230 national gene banks and a number of research centers that relied on international cooperation. Today, international organizations help fund gene banks, support education concerning the ins and outs of genetic conservation, and coordinate communication and exchange among the world's gene banks.

Keeping Seeds

Unfortunately, seeds don't last forever in storage, and some kinds of seeds keep better than others. If kept at room temperature, for example, corn seeds are only good for a few years, while tomato seeds will keep much longer without losing their ability to germinate. Seeds of barley and oats 123 years old have still sprouted, while lettuce seed can completely die out in just a year under even slightly moist conditions. Cold storage can dramatically improve seed survival. Although only a little over a third of well-dried lettuce seeds survives eight years of storage at 90°F (32°C), 93 percent lasts at least nineteen years if stored below freezing.

When the NSSL was first established, the seeds were kept at a temperature just above freezing. But that wasn't cold enough. The seeds didn't keep well, and some lost their ability to germinate and grow. In the 1970s, in response to concerns about loss of diversity, the NSSL was upgraded for long-term storage at lower temperatures, around 0°F (−20°C). But even that temperature turned out to result in the deterioration of the genetic material, especially of crops with short-lived seeds.

When the seeds begin to lose their viability—their ability to germinate and grow in a healthy fashion—all is not lost. A portion of the sample can be planted, tended, and harvested, yielding fresh new seeds that can in turn be stored for a number of years. But when a seed bank is trying to maintain diversity by storing tens of thousands of samples, reducing the frequency of planting out becomes critical. Planting requires a great deal of land, the attention of many gardeners, and the use of resources such as water. The longer seeds can be stored, the more practical it is to keep an abundant variety and preserve them properly.

Seeds of most crop plants can withstand very cold temperatures. At the NSSL, about half the storage space is devoted to steel tanks, about five feet in diameter and three feet tall. The bottom of each tank is filled with liquid nitrogen, which exists at a temperature of about −300°F (−196°C). Each tank has a rack suspended above the nitrogen that can hold approximately 2,500 seed samples, each within its own labeled container. The temperature in the nitrogen vapor where the seeds are kept is about −256°F (−160°C). Chemical activity within seeds comes to a virtual standstill at such low temperatures, slowing deterioration to almost nothing. Scientists believe seeds can last from one hundred to five hundred years under such liquid nitrogen cryostorage. Where once samples had to be tested every five years to see if they were still healthy, now they only need to be tested every ten years. Because each test of viability uses up a portion of the sample, reducing the frequency of testing is very important.

Not all seeds can tolerate liquid nitrogen storage. When new samples are brought to the NSSL, about fifty seeds are frozen in liquid nitrogen for twenty-four hours. Then they are planted side by side with an equal number of seeds that weren't frozen. If the test indicates that the seeds won't tolerate the cold, they are stored at −20°F (0°C) instead.

Saving Diversity in the United States

The United States is especially concerned with preserving crop diversity for many reasons. But perhaps the most important is that all our major crops originated elsewhere. North America has contributed some delicious foods such as strawberries, blueberries, and pecans to the world's diet. But the foods people rely on for their basic diet, for survival, are grains—corn, wheat, and rice in particular. Corn developed closest to home, in Mexico and Central America. But that important crop lacks wild relatives in the United States, and most of the land races cultivated by Native Americans have died out. Wheat and rice evolved in Asia. Other important crops also began elsewhere—potatoes in South America, beans in Mexico and the Andes, tomatoes in Mexico, onions in Asia, and the cabbage family in the Mediterranean. Even our favorite fruits such as apples and peaches got their start in faraway Asia. We have no native genetic reserves of any major crops to fall back on. Because everything comes from somewhere else, it is critical for American agriculture that we collect and preserve diversity from the rest of the world.

Americans have always been interested in plant diversity. George Washington and Thomas Jefferson were both scientific farmers interested in new species and varieties. As Jefferson said in 1790, "The greatest service which can be rendered any country is to add a useful plant to its culture." Even before America became a country, Benjamin Franklin was sending home seeds and plant cuttings from England, where he served as Pennsylvania's ambassador. In 1836, the Patent Office began sending introduced seeds to American farmers, and new plants began being cataloged officially in 1898 with the introduction of a cabbage from Russia. It was given PI (Plant Introduction) Number 1. Since then, more than 400,000 PIs have been added to the list.

The U.S. National Plant Germplasm System coordinates the preservation of plant genetic diversity in the United States. It is a network of federal, state, and private organizations that cooperate in preserving, evaluating, and cataloging plant germplasm, or genetic material, that is collected around the world. Each part of the system has its own particular part to play in the preservation process.

The NSSL is the long-term seed storage facility. Here, backup samples of all the seed samples are kept to guard against losses from disease or disaster elsewhere in the system. The rooms containing the samples are enclosed within a thick-walled vault that can withstand a seven-foot flood, a tornado with force equal to a four thousand-pound automobile propelled at 120 mph, or an earthquake so strong it would be expected to occur only once in ten thousand years. Careful security measures protect the collection from the possibility of terrorism or vandalism.

The four Regional Plant Introduction Stations store thousands of species and varieties and distribute germplasm to research scientists. In addition to the stations, smaller working collections, such as the National Potato Introduction Station in Wisconsin, concentrate on one crop or type of crop. In addition, ten National Clonal Germplasm Repositories preserve fruits, nuts, and landscape varieties as living plants. Altogether, germplasm is stored in twenty-six locations across the country, from Geneva, New York, to Hilo, Hawaii, as well as in Puerto Rico. The National Germplasm Resources Laboratory in Beltsville, Maryland, coordinates plant exploration activities and arranges for exchanges of germplasm with other countries, while the National Plant Germplasm Quarantine Center in Glenn Dale, Maryland, checks out samples to make sure they are free of pests that could damage American crops.

Keeping Everything Straight

The NSSL stores approximately 300,000 genetically different samples from about 2,000 plant species, with thousands more added each year. Each sample contains about 5,000 seeds. In addition, the regional stations, clonal repositories, and working collections also have samples. The amount of information about each sample varies, and new information may be obtained when a scientist studies a particular variety. All this material must be organized so that a particular sample and information about it can be easily found. The U.S. National Plant Germplasm System has developed a very efficient way of evaluating, preparing, and storing seeds and of filing information.

When a sample arrives at the NSSL, it is kept at 41°F (5°C) in the seed equilibrium room until it can be tested. There, bags, jars, and boxes of seeds lie on shelves awaiting evaluation. Each sample is given a number, which is logged onto the system's computer. Each gets a bar-code label so it can be rapidly identified.

The seeds are cleaned in the seed conditioning room; many arrive mixed with dirt or dead plant parts, especially those collected in the wild or in farmers' fields in remote areas. Then they are tested for germination in walk-in germination chambers. These bleak rooms have walls with banks of fluorescent lights and rolling airtight shelved chambers in which proper humidity can be maintained. The heat and humidity make the germination chambers feel like a sauna, but the conditions are perfect for the seeds.'

Before being stored, the seeds are also tested for moisture content, which should be below 6 percent. They are then sealed in moisture-proof bags for conventional storage or in long plastic tubes for cryostorage.

Information about each sample—species, where and when collected, germination rate, possibly valuable characteristics, and so on—is entered into the system's computer network. Through an access program called GRIN (Germplasm Resources Information Network), researchers and plant breeders around the world can search through the entries about all the samples from their offices by telephone, using a computer modem. The GRIN system is headquartered at the resource center in Beltsville, but information can be added to it by any of the facilities in the system. A breeder who decides a sample might possess characteristics he or she is looking for can request seeds. The results of any evaluations of the samples—for disease resistance, crop quality, drought resistance, or whatever—are entered into the GRIN system. Yearly, the various collections in the system send out almost 200,000 samples to users in the United States and more than a hundred other countries.

Problem Plants

The seeds of tropical crops such as cocoa and mangos present a difficulty for seed banks. Such plants evolved in parts of the world where there is no winter. Their seeds normally begin to grow soon after they are deposited on the ground and have not had to adapt to a cold season during which they have to remain dormant. They survive only a few weeks to several months before dying if not planted. Scientists at seed banks are trying to find ways of storing these seeds.

Tropical seeds aren't the only troublemakers for seed storage facilities. Potatoes need to be planted each year to keep them going. Fruit tree seeds can't be practically planted out for regeneration—it takes years for them to grow from seed and produce seed-bearing fruit. So scientists are studying other ways of preserving genetic diversity besides saving seeds.

One way of capturing and keeping genes is to collect pollen. Since pollen is carried from one plant to another by animals or by the wind, it must be able to withstand at least some drying. That makes it a candidate for storage. The NSSL is also experimenting with cryostorage of apple buds. If they keep well, the buds could be grafted onto orchard trees when needed to produce branches of the desired variety.

Maintaining Diversity

Vital as gene banks are to preserving diversity, they also have serious problems. Their purpose may be to maintain diversity, but unless gene-bank managers are very careful, they can drastically reduce the diversity they are trying to protect in the process of preserving it. It is all too easy for a new variation on evolution to take hold—adaptation to survival under the conditions of a gene bank! This can happen in several ways that need to be understood if the problems are to be minimized.

We've learned that much of the value of land races and wild species lies in the diversity each carries within itself. That is, unlike a uniform high-yield variety developed by researchers, a land race or wild species carries a variety of alleles in its gene pool. The larger the sample of seeds, the greater the likelihood that a healthy range of alleles will be included. Sampling the same species or race over a wide geographic range also helps ensure that valuable diversity is preserved.

Once samples have been collected, labeled, and stored, it is vitally important that they are maintained in ways that continue to preserve their genetic variability. Deciding how often to plant out samples to renew the seeds is critical. In order to maintain seed quality, the stored samples are periodically tested for their ability to germinate. When a certain percentage of the seeds do not germinate, the sample is planted out to obtain fresh seeds that can be stored again.

But even seeds that will germinate in tests may have begun to deteriorate in ways that affect the diversity of the sample. Old seeds may result in abnormal seedlings, weak plants that don't grow well, or plants that produce seeds poorly. And not all seeds in one sample may tolerate storage as well as others. When genes are close together on a chromosome, they tend to stay together during the formation of the egg and sperm cells. Such genes are said to be "linked" to one another. If seeds are stored too long between plantings, potentially useful genes linked to genes that result in poor ability to survive in storage will be lost. Researcher Eric Roos of the NSSL studied this problem during the 1970s using beans. He artificially aged the beans from eight varieties in a way that simulated storage. After a number of treatments, half the varieties lost their ability to germinate altogether. Thus, half the diversity in his sample was lost. Unfortunately, the inability to produce healthy plants after long storage can be linked to the kinds of traits that modern breeders want to preserve, such as resistance to diseases.

But planting out is a laborious process requiring land, water, and plenty of attention. Gene-bank managers must make decisions that balance the rate of deterioration against the practicality of planting out. If the intervals between plantings are too long, some diversity will be lost as seeds lose their viability in storage. But it is impossible to plant out tens of thousands of samples every year.

The process of planting out itself can imperil diversity. Roos simulated the process of storage and planting out using bean varieties of different shapes and colors. That way, just from looking at the seeds he harvested he could get an idea of how much diversity was lost over time. He aged the beans, planted them, and harvested the resulting seeds, then aged, planted, and harvested again for a total of fifteen cycles. When he was finished, all the seeds were the same color, but two shapes remained. Six of the eight varieties he had started with were gone as a result of being treated as if they were being kept in a gene bank. He had plenty of seeds, but they were seeds that had evolved to be adapted to gene-bank conditions, not to the kinds of environments they had lived in before being subjected to "preservation."

Choosing how many seeds to plant is critical. If too few are planted, some potentially valuable genes could be left out just by chance. The genes would be lost forever, with no one ever even knowing they were there. And every time the sample was planted out, more genetic variety would be lost through this random choice of seeds to plant. Over a number of generations, an alarming amount of diversity would be lost, as Roos showed with his different-colored beans.

Once the seeds are planted, still more problems arise. Some seeds germinate more rapidly than others. The plants from those seeds can get a head start in the field and shade out or otherwise out-compete slower ones. Remember, preserving diversity means saving the "weak" as well as the "strong"; a genotype that germinates slowly could possess other potentially valuable traits. Caretakers of fields where seed banks renew their samples need to watch for such variation in germination.

Another important way plants can vary is in when and how they produce their seeds. Caretakers must plant different varieties of the same crop far enough from one another to avoid cross-pollination. This problem can be especially tricky with corn, since the wind can carry corn pollen for more than a mile. In addition, some seeds may be ready for harvest well in advance of others. When Roos tested one bean sample, he found that some of the plants flowered in forty-seven days while others took seventy-four days to blossom. If caretakers only gather seeds once or twice, plants that produce either very early or very late could be missed. Collecting the seeds carefully over a period of time until seeds from all plants have been included is very important in preserving diversity.

Other problems with maintaining the genetic assortment of gene-bank samples cannot be controlled. Seeds collected in the New Mexican desert might not grow well in the climate of northern Colorado, for example. A land race from halfway around the world may turn out to be very susceptible to a disease prevalent in the region of the gene bank and could even die off completely when planted out. Crop failure due to extreme weather conditions such as an untimely frost can also wipe out an attempt to renew seeds that have been in storage. Even with careful management, gene banks just cannot preserve all of the diversity that existed when the plants were growing in their original environments and producing seeds each year under natural conditions.

Frozen in Time

Another subtle difficulty haunts the whole concept of gene banks. Seeds kept in storage for many years between plantings and then planted in a protected environment, far from the cultivated fields where their usefulness could someday lie, are suspended in time, separate from the forces of evolution that shape all living things. If the plants were reproducing out in the world, their genetic makeup would not remain static. They would be constantly evolving to adapt to their changing environment. But when the seeds are safely stored away, they are isolated from the environment. They are not exposed to the pests and diseases that are always evolving out in the world and finding new ways of getting around the defenses that plants develop against them.

Plants that live out their lives each year and produce their seeds evolve along with these new threats to their survival by developing new defenses against the ever-changing threats in their environment. Plants protected within seed banks are cushioned from such harsh reality. Pests and diseases aren't the only dangers. People are quickly changing the conditions on the planet. Ultraviolet radiation, which can damage living things, is increasing, for example, and pollutants in the environment are building up. The atmosphere may be warming due to the greenhouse effect. We can hope that these increases are slow enough so that plants and animals in nature can adapt and develop ways to protect themselves. But gene-bank plants that are only exposed over intervals of years to the earth's environment are not getting the opportunity to evolve along with changing conditions.

Continuity in Collections

Many of the most valuable collections of genetic diversity were gathered by scientists deeply involved with just one species or a group of related species. Unless the collection has been carefully organized, with everything labeled in a way anyone can understand, it becomes just about useless once that person dies. Improper storage can also be a problem for such collections. Much precious diversity has disappeared in this way, including Mangelsdorf's corn collection. Although we don't know for sure, scientists fear that much of Vavilov's material has been lost over the years, despite the dedication of institute workers during the war. And many less-developed countries lack funds for maintaining important collections, so numerous samples have deteriorated and land races have been lost.

A great deal of planning goes into a successful seed bank. Curators need to be trained on the job so they can learn the pitfalls firsthand. In some jobs, mistakes by the inexperienced are not serious. But in a seed bank, just a year or two of mistakes can result in a massive loss of diversity. Up to now seed banks have emphasized acquiring and storing samples. This is understandable given the rapid decline in cultivation of locally adapted land races and the massive destruction of wild places. But a seed bank also needs to evaluate its samples as they come in, regenerate them carefully, and make them available to breeders who need them. The NSSL has procedures for expediting these activities, but unfortunately many seed banks in the world do not.

The social turmoil in the world today endangers efforts to save genetic diversity through seed banks. Scientists are concerned about the fate of the Russian collection, one of the largest in the world. The breakup of the Soviet Union resulted in many financial problems for the Russian government, and no one is sure whether the Vavilov Institute will receive adequate funding to protect its collection. There are fewer employees to plant out seeds and tubers, and the compressors that provide backup cold storage are unreliable. Meanwhile, other seed collections that were under Soviet control are now located in what have become different countries—Ukraine and Belarus, for example. Their fate remains to be seen.

The first scientist to systematically collect genetic diversity from around the world was the Russian Nikolai Vavilov, who founded the Vavilov Institute in Leningrad. Drawing on the disciplines of botany, geography, and genetics, Vavilov was the first scientist to devise a coherent theory that attempted to explain the origins of and variations in the world's crop plants.

During the 1920s and 1930s, Vavilov visited more than fifty countries on five continents, traveling overland into isolated regions to collect over sixty thousand samples of plants. Other collectors sent seeds and tubers to Vavilov, making his institute the most important repository for crop plant varieties and their wild relatives in the world. The material he collected was evaluated for potential uses in improving crops and was made available to breeders.

Up Close:
THE FIRST GREAT COLLECTOR

Vavilov developed a theory concerning the origins of domesticated plants. He believed that the greatest variety in a particular crop, such as corn, would be found close to the place where it originated. By plotting the diversity he found on his travels, Vavilov developed maps showing where he thought the different species were first domesticated. While his theories have been modified by other researchers over time, Vavilov's maps are still used to pinpoint some regions of diversity.

Vavilov found that a number of crops including soybeans, peaches, apricots, and oranges showed their greatest diversity in China. He designated India as a center for rice, cucumbers, and eggplants, while peas, certain kinds of wheat, apples, and carrots were especially diverse in central Asia. The Near East is clearly a center of diversity for other

By going to the places where crops were first grown, collectors like Vavilov have been able to collect many varieties and species of crops such as beans.

PHOTO BY DAVID CAVAGNARO

kinds of wheat as well as for rye, melons, almonds, and grapes. Cabbage, lettuce, and olives seem to have originated in the Mediterranean region. Sweet potatoes, potatoes, tomatoes, and lima beans started out along the Pacific coast of South America, whereas Mexico and Central America are home to the beginnings of peppers, squash, common beans, and corn.

At the height of his career, Vavilov was in charge of four hundred research stations span-ning the USSR that employed twenty thousand people. Unfortunately for Vavilov and for Russia, he fell out of favor with the Communist dictator Joseph Stalin in 1940. Stalin needed someone to blame for the failure of his push to collectivize farming. Vavilov, who aroused suspicion because of his extensive travels abroad, was the chosen scapegoat. Stalin had Vavilov arrested for "spying and agricultural sabotage" and put in prison, where he starved to death in 1942.

CHAPTER NINE

PEOPLE PRESERVING
PLANT DIVERSITY

Governments and international agencies aren't the only entities concerned about loss of genetic diversity. Private citizens, many of them expert gardeners, have experienced the loss of diversity on a personal scale, noticing with alarm the disappearance of favorite varieties from mail order seed catalogs. They have also seen family favorites pass away along with the old-time gardeners who kept them alive. Some home gardeners have banded together in different ways to help stop the genetic erosion of American gardens.

Home Garden Needs

The needs of a home gardener are much different from those of a professional farmer. Consider tomatoes. A commercial tomato variety must ship easily. That means it has to be firm in texture and have a tough skin. Flavor is a secondary consideration. Commercial varieties also should ripen all their fruit at the same time so they can be harvested all at once. Home gardeners, however, want tasty, tender, juicy tomatoes. Unless they are doing a lot of home canning, they also prefer that the fruits ripen intermittently over a longer season. That way, the gardener can walk out to the garden, pick a couple of ripe tomatoes at the peak of flavor, and add them to the evening's salad.

Because home gardening is popular in the United States, there is some demand for varieties that suit its needs. But commercial farming is a much bigger business, so most breeding efforts are geared to agriculture rather

Previous page: Tomatoes come in an abundant variety of colors, sizes, and shapes, only a few of which are shown here. PHOTO COURTESY OF USDA

than gardening. In addition, governments in major agricultural states such as California carry out ambitious breeding programs targeted toward commercial crops.

Gardening can be especially tricky for people who don't live in the vast midwestern region, where the climate is similar for stretches of hundreds of miles. Most commercially developed varieties are adapted to this area or to the Central Valley of California, since that is where most farms are. Gardeners who struggle to produce home crops in the hot, sandy desert; in a northern mountain valley; or in the cool, wet Pacific Northwest must choose what they grow very carefully. And seed catalogs, especially in recent years as family-owned seed companies have been bought by multinational corporations, often don't carry regionally adapted varieties. Instead of striving to serve a diverse public, most companies now offer only the varieties that sell best, trimming their catalogs until they appeal most to gardeners in the American heartland, where most of the gardening public lives.

Seed Savers Exchange

When Kent Whealy accepted the seeds of a small purple morning glory, a productive climbing bean, and a large pink tomato from his wife's grandfather, Baptist Ott, he had no idea where this small act of preservation would lead. Kent and Diane Whealy were recently married, and the old man had shared some of his gardening tricks with the young couple as they planted their first garden together. In the fall of 1974, he gave them samples of these three favorites that had come from Bavaria, Germany, four generations ago.

When Ott died that winter, Whealy knew the only way these three unusual plants would continue was for him to plant the seeds. He began to wonder how many other old gardeners had died, leaving perhaps unplanted seeds behind with no one to continue to propagate them. It seemed a terrible loss for well-loved, beautiful, and useful plants to disappear just because no one knew about them.

Whealy decided to find out if other people shared his concern and founded the Seed Savers Exchange in 1975. He wrote letters to gardening magazines and back-to-the-land publications, asking others to join him. At first, the response was disappointing. But soon the idea caught on, and now the Seed Savers Exchange is a thriving organization that preserves thousands of garden varieties not offered in seed catalogs.

Every year, Seed Savers issues the *Seed Savers Yearbook*, which lists the names and addresses of about nine hundred members who are offering vegetable seeds or cuttings from fruit trees to other members. More than six thousand different heirloom varieties are available in this way. Seed Savers also publishes guides on how to save seeds and how to ensure that the varieties saved remain pure. Since 1975, Seed Savers members have distributed over half a million samples, many of them seriously endangered varieties that probably would have died out otherwise.

Some scientists are skeptical about backyard gardeners preserving genetic diversity. They don't believe that such a loose system can result in reliable results, or that some of the material is even worth saving. They think that seed

banks, with their modern storage techniques and their
carefully planned grow-outs, can do the job. But the diversity of crop plants is so wonderfully abundant, despite
all the losses, that gene banks can't do the whole job. In
1985, a study commissioned by Congress found that of the
1,799 heirloom varieties being conserved by Seed Savers,
only 147 were stocked in government collections. Seed
Savers had 544 kinds of tomatoes; the government had
just 133 of them. Only 3 percent of the vegetable varieties
offered in seed catalogs in 1903 were being preserved by
the NSSL. Many of these were being protected by Seed
Savers. Many of the varieties in the NSSL, in turn, were
not available from Seed Savers. Both Seed Savers and the
NSSL are playing important roles in preserving the precious diversity of the foods we depend on for survival.

The Nancy watermelon is an example of a once-
popular variety brought back to life by Seed Savers. Its
green-striped, twenty-five-pound fruit was discovered
growing in a Georgia cotton field by Nancy Tate in the
1800s. Some seeds of this delicious drought- and disease-
resistant melon were taken by a relative to Arkansas,
where it provided part of the foundation of a major melon-
growing industry. But as time went on, commercial growers switched to hybrids with thick rinds that made them
preferable for shipping, and the Nancy fell from favor.
Family members kept growing it, but it almost disappeared. In 1986, the Nancy was rescued when a family
member who remembered it but didn't grow the melon
got some seeds from Nancy Tate's seventy-eight-year-old
son. In 1991, the Nancy became available again to the

watermelon-loving public through Southern Exposure Seed Exchange, which specializes in heirloom varieties adapted to hot, humid climates.

Seeds for Sale

In addition to maintaining a network of backyard gardeners who perpetuate varieties that can't be bought from catalogs, Seed Savers keeps track of the American gardening industry's seed diversity, publishing a *Garden Seed Inventory* (third edition, 1992) that lets people know where to obtain seeds for thousands of varieties of plants ranging from popular crops such as beans to more obscure ones such as amaranth, an ancient American grain.

The *Garden Seed Inventory* lists every nonhybrid vegetable variety available from U.S. or Canadian seed companies. Not only does the *Garden Seed Inventory* help gardeners locate seeds for unusual varieties, it also contains information that is invaluable to gardeners who are concerned with the takeover of small seed companies and the increasing prevalence of hybrids among seed offerings. Statistics in the *Inventory* show that from 1984 to 1991, almost half of the nonhybrid varieties offered in mail-order catalogs had been dropped. By choosing to buy the nonhybrids that are still available and by patronizing the smaller suppliers, gardeners can support diversity with their dollars.

The *Garden Seed Inventory* is packed with information to help both the home gardener and the cause of maintaining diversity. Each listing gives a brief description of the variety's characteristics, strengths, and weaknesses, followed by a tally of how many seed companies offered it in pre-

vious years. Lastly, the names of companies currently selling the seeds are given. By studying the listings, a gardener
can see which varieties are gaining in popularity and
which seem about to disappear completely from catalogs.
That way, gardeners can choose to grow varieties adapted
to their areas that are in danger of vanishing. Since Seed
Savers only concerns itself with open-pollinated varieties,
gardeners can keep a variety going in their own gardens
by saving seeds if it disappears from commercial sources.

The trends plotted by Seed Savers in the *Garden Seed
Inventory* are both hopeful and worrisome. Between 1987
and 1991, for example, 1,263 varieties disappeared from
seed catalogs. But over the same time period, 1,753 were
added. It is sad to see varieties disappear, but it is heart-
ening to see others added, many of which aren't "new"
at all but instead represent heirloom varieties that have
been rescued and then offered to the public. Unfortunately, many of the newly available varieties may not last
long because 1,411 of them, or more than 80 percent, were
offered by only one seed company. If that catalog dropped
a variety, it would disappear from the marketplace.

Of the 1,411 varieties offered by only one company,
more than half were available from one of sixteen companies that are especially concerned with preserving diversity. Some of these are commercial ventures run by
concerned people. Others are branches of organizations
that serve the cause of diversity in other ways besides selling seeds.

A preservation group called Native Seeds/SEARCH
was the only source for 83 of the newly listed varieties in
1991 as well as for 125 others not available anywhere else.

This group focuses on Native American varieties in particular—various types of corn, squash, chiles, and sunflowers, for example. The founders of the group appreciate that heirloom seeds often provide more than just food—they come with symbolic meanings, interesting stories, and special means of cultivation. Native Seeds/SEARCH is concerned with the social heritage that goes along with seeds. It makes an effort to uncover the origins of the varieties and to preserve and to document any cultural uses associated with them. Since it began in the early 1980s, this organization has helped return seeds to more than a dozen Indian reservations in the Southwest as well as to many communities in Mexico.

Saving Fruit Diversity

Maintaining the genetic diversity of fruits presents its own problems. Most fruits grow on trees, which take many years of growth before producing fruit. It is completely impractical to save fruit-tree seeds in a gene bank and plant them out periodically. Tree fruit varieties can only be properly preserved as living trees.

The number of fruit varieties grown commercially in the United States is pitifully small. Somewhere between 8,000 and 10,000 named varieties of apples have been recorded. But today, only twelve to fifteen varieties make up 95 percent of the commercial apple crop, and only about a hundred old and new varieties are grown for sale in total. Like vegetables, fruit grown for shipment to market must be firm and have a tough skin to avoid bruising. Fruit has to keep well on the grocery counter while waiting to be bought, and it must look attractive to the customer. But just like vegetables, different fruit varieties have an array of distinctive genetic traits relating to time of harvest, quality and properties of the fruit, and susceptibility to pests and diseases. Only by saving this diversity rather than limiting ourselves to a few commercial varieties can we hope to keep enjoying quality fruit for generations to come.

Fortunately, fruits have a big advantage when it comes to preserving diversity. More than one variety can be grown on the same tree through the process of grafting. In grafting, a small piece from one tree is joined to another tree by tightly taping the two together. The grafted material becomes part of the tree and grows with it. In this way, one tree can produce dozens of different varieties. The only problem is that if the tree itself dies for some reason, all the material grafted to it dies as well.

Old and interesting fruit varieties have enthusiastic fans. Many heirloom fruits have traits such as easy bruising, uneven shape, poor color, or unattractive skin that make them undesirable for supermarket sales. But old varieties were often developed for the most important fruit trait—flavor—and people who love fruits and have the time and space to grow them are in for some special taste treats. In 1967, some of these fruit lovers banded together to form the North American Fruit Explorers (NAFEX). This organization includes scientists, professional nursery growers, and amateur orchardists, all of whom share a love of fine fruit. They communicate with one another through a journal that contains articles on promising varieties and unusual fruits. Members also exchange samples of varieties with one another, sharing twigs that can be grafted so many can enjoy and preserve rare and wonderful varieties. NAFEX members have a number of special interests, all of which contribute to maintaining the diversity of fruits. Some specialize in less-familiar species such as papaws and mayhaws, while others strive to develop disease-resistant varieties of familiar fruits such as apples. Others grow their fruits under difficult conditions or on the margins of the normal climatic region where that fruit thrives. Some of them insist on using organic methods and shun chemicals, while others don't mind spraying their trees so they can get an unblemished harvest.

Theo Grootendorst of Southmeadow Fruit Gardens in Lakeside, Michigan, uses another approach to foster the genetic diversity of North American fruits. He offers more than 250 apple varieties as well as over 200 kinds of apricots, cherries, currants, grapes, nectarines, pears, peaches, plums, and lesser-known fruits for sale to the public. All his varieties have been selected because of their fine flavor rather than because they look good or ship well. Few people have heard of apples such as Calville Blanc d'Hiver, a tender, spicy dessert apple that has more vitamin C than an orange, or Oldmixon Free peach, the earliest recorded American peach, which has large, white-fleshed, very juicy fruit and was prized by Thomas Jefferson. But they are among Southmeadow's offerings.

Heirloom Pitfalls

Saving the wonderful diversity of garden crops and fruits is an important goal. But this activity complements other methods of preservation such as seed banks. When wild species and land races are gathered and stored properly in seed banks, abundant diversity is saved. Much of that diversity cannot be seen in the external appearance of the plants. It involves hidden physiological processes within the plant that determine important survival tactics such as disease resistance, cold tolerance, and plant vigor.

The garden varieties we grow, however, are mainly distinguished from one another by obvious visual characteristics. One kind of tomato may have a compact growth habit, potatolike leaves, and medium-size yellow fruits, while another may have a rambling way of growing, more finely divided tomato-style leaves, and large red fruit. The two seem very different to us, yet they may differ from one another in only a few of their thousands of genes. Despite differences in their external appearance, their genetic heritage may be quite similar. In contrast, as we've seen, corn seed that looks similar can produce very diversely adapted plants.

C H A P T E R   T E N

PEOPLE PRESERVING
ANIMAL DIVERSITY

reserving rare animal breeds and wild relatives of domesticated animals is such a low priority worldwide that precious few efforts are being made to keep these creatures from dying out. We already have seen the tragedy of such losses. When white men came to southern Africa, vast herds of an unusual zebra called the quagga roamed the plains. Unlike familiar zebras, the quagga was basically a reddish tan color, with striping limited to the front part of the body. Within a period of forty years, starting in 1840 when travelers described vast herds of these unique animals, they were completely wiped out in the wild. The last zoo specimen died in Amsterdam in 1883.

Loss of any wild species at human hands is a tragedy. But the possibility of an easier life in Africa may have accompanied the quagga's demise. Zebras in general are immune to the disease-carrying tsetse fly, a killer that keeps people and domesticated animals at bay over much of southern Africa. Horses cannot be used in these regions, for they easily sicken and die. But while zebras are immune to the tsetse, they are difficult to tame and are not suited as working companions for humans. The quagga, however, was said by some to have been more gentle and less "wild" than other zebras. It might have been tamable, or perhaps it could have been crossbred with horses to produce a disease-resistant hybrid that could have been used on farms. We will never know.

More recently, popular animal breeds have disap-

The Gloucester Old Spot pig is a rare old breed that can take care of itself. PHOTO BY DOROTHY H. PATENT

peared in just a few generations. Only later have people realized that those now-extinct breeds could have proved useful in previously unforeseen ways. The appealing, curly-coated Lincolnshire pig was the lean and hearty common pig of the nineteenth century. But in the early twentieth century, the public demanded well-marbled tender pork chops and fatty bacon that fried up crisp. The Lincolnshire was the loser in this popularity contest and disappeared in 1967. Now, people know that fatty meat is not good for them. Modern life involves little hard labor, and people need low-fat diets to be healthy. The lean Lincolnshire might have been the perfect source for the genes pigs need today to satisfy modern preferences.

Saving Minor Breeds

In North America, eighty of our 175 livestock breeds are considered in danger of extinction. For some of these, only a handful of individuals remain. Not all of them are exotic or obscure breeds we've never heard of, either—cattle including the familiar Guernsey, once a favorite as the family-farm milk cow, are threatened.

Thanks largely to men like John Bender, whose Mokelumne River Ranch harbors twenty-four breeds of livestock as well as a number of kinds of barnyard birds, much of the wonderful diversity of domesticated animals is being preserved. Bender belongs to the American Livestock Breeds Conservancy (ALBC), an organization devoted to celebrating the variety of farm animals. Founded in 1977, the ALBC has grown from 150 to more than 3,000 members, all of whom are concerned about the loss of genetic diversity in our domesticated animals.

The ALBC is the only institution in the United States dedicated to conserving rare breeds of domesticated animals. It provides a way for breeders and breed associations to be in touch with one another so they can know what is going on in other parts of the country and can find out who may have animals of particular breeds. The conservancy has breed registries for minor breeds, performs censuses that help determine which breeds are in greatest danger of extinction, and has set up a semen bank for rare cattle breeds. Its list of breeders of rare animals also helps buyers find breeding stock and serves as a market for breeders.

In addition, the ALBC has designed a data bank of livestock breeds for the USDA that parallels the USDA's plant data bank. Now animal scientists worldwide can access information on breeds and breed characteristics because the information in the bank has been made available internationally through the United Nations Food and Agriculture Organization.

In Great Britain, the Rare Breeds Survival Trust plays a role similar to that of the ALBC. Britain is home to many breeds of cattle, pigs, sheep, and poultry that developed in different valleys and villages. Most breeds popular in the United States, such as Hereford cattle or Suffolk sheep, derive their names from the regions of the British Isles where they originated. The Rare Breeds Survival Trust evaluates breeds to determine their strengths and weaknesses and tries to educate people about advantages such as high-quality meat or easy calving. When only a few individuals of a breed survive, inbreeding can become a problem. The Rare Breeds Survival Trust keeps pedigree records that help breeders make decisions about which animals to mate to avoid inbreeding as much as possible.

In some countries, such as Hungary and Brazil, the government runs farms for preserving rare livestock. In France, money from registries for commercially raised cattle is used to track down rare breeds and collect semen for cryogenic storage. Switzerland has an unusual private preservation group that has bought up rare breed stock for all species except cattle. Now, it "rents" these animals to farmers who, in turn, breed the animals carefully. The United Nations has begun to see the importance of saving rare breeds and is asking for livestock surveys from countries around the world in an attempt to find out just what is out there, especially in Third World countries.

Making Money from Rare Breeds

Saving unusual animals can be very satisfying. But animals are expensive to keep and take up plenty of space. Few people can afford to keep rare breeds just for the satisfaction of knowing they are doing a good deed. They must also somehow be able to make a living. One obvious way is to sell excess animals. Some uncommon breeds, especially small-size ones, are popular with people with country homes. In general, female animals are more important in conserving rare breeds, since one male can mate with a number of females. Excess males can be sold as pets or for their meat, and both males and females that are good examples of the breed can be sold as breeding stock. If a breeder is lucky, the discovery of valuable traits in a breed he or she raises can mean good prices.

Farm parks are an excellent way to combine bringing in some money with educating the public about the importance of rare breeds and the appealing nature of such interesting animals. Farm parks charge an entry fee, just like an amusement park or a zoo. People can walk around to visit the different animals, perhaps feeding ducks in a pond and having a family picnic in beautiful surroundings. Children can pet young animals, and the whole family can learn something about the history of agriculture firsthand while having a good time. John Bender, for one, is landscaping his Mokelumne River Ranch as a farm park.

Saving Wild Relatives

While botanists comb wild places near the centers of origin of crop plants to collect and preserve as many wild relatives as possible, little is done to protect or study the wild relatives of domesticated animals. Shortsighted as this may be, it is somewhat understandable. First of all, it is much easier to collect plant specimens and to preserve seeds than to find, capture, and keep wild animals. Breeding plants is relatively simple and inexpensive compared to breeding animals—plants don't need to be fed and sheltered, and a large number can be reproduced on a small amount of land. Although seeds take up little space and can usually be stored for a number of years if necessary, animals take up plenty of space and must be constantly fed, even when they are not breeding. And finally, crop plants lie at the base of the food chain—everyone eats plant foods, and we could not survive without them. Animals are important in providing working power and dietary protein, but humankind could survive on a purely

141

vegetarian diet. Still, animal foods are an important part of the human diet, and much more could be done to study the potential usefulness of wild relatives without great effort and expense. Many of these creatures live in zoos around the world; perhaps cooperative efforts between those zoos and livestock scientists could be developed.

Zoos used to be little more than places where people went to look at animals from faraway lands that lived boring lives in barred cages. But in recent years, zoos have been transformed into much more pleasant environments for wild things and into important centers for breeding animals that are rare or extinct in the wild. Some of these creatures, relatives of domesticated animals, possess potentially valuable traits.

When species are endangered in the wild, increasing their populations in captivity can be vital to their survival. Maintaining the genetic diversity within captive species is critical, for inbreeding can lead to infertility and high mortality. But crossing animals that have different genetic heritages may involve mating animals that live half a world apart. In addition, many animals bear only a single offspring each year, so increases in numbers are slow. In the modern zoo, scientists work to get around such limitations of nature.

The gaur, a threatened relative of cattle, was among the first animals on which new techniques were tried. The gaur, a massive beast that can stand more than six feet tall at the shoulder, lives in India, Nepal, and southeast Asia. Like so many wild species, they are threatened with extinction because their habitat is being destroyed and because they are hunted. Long ago, gaur were domesticated and evolved into the mithan, a useful draft and meat animal. In Bhutan, mithan are crossed with cattle to produce a productive milk animal. It is clear that the gaur might possess valuable traits it could contribute to domesticated livestock.

In 1981, an embryo from a female gaur was transplanted into the uterus of a common Holstein cow. A healthy male calf was born at the Bronx Zoo, the first wild mammal in the world to have a domestic surrogate mother. Embryos of domesticated cattle routinely are frozen, transported to faraway destinations, and implanted into cows that have given birth successfully. Frozen cattle semen also is used regularly with consistent success. We can hope that such methods become routine in zoo breeding as well.

Techniques such as embryo transplantation and artificial insemination can be very helpful in wildlife conservation for a number of reasons. Animals are subject to stress from travel—anytime an animal is handled and transported, its health is at risk. Endangered animals are extremely valuable, and just one individual might represent a critical amount of genetic variability for the species. In addition, animals can carry diseases that could infect others at the destination zoo. These problems could be avoided if semen and embryos could be reliably frozen and transported around the world.

FINDING
CREATIVE SOLUTIONS

P reservation of genetic diversity sometimes looks like a losing battle. So many forces are acting against this goal that it can seem to be a lost cause. But if enough people realize the importance of maintaining diversity and do what they can to promote it, a significant amount of the abundant variations of our cultivated crops and domesticated animals can continue to exist.

Pluses and Minuses

Each method of saving diversity has its drawbacks, but each has strengths as well. Despite their problems, gene banks are a powerful tool for storing an enormous amount of diversity in very compact quarters. They encourage cooperation between governments and private breeders around the world, which is critical for maintaining diversity and for utilizing valuable genes in practical ways. Saving heirloom varieties may sometimes seem to focus on maintaining the status quo by an emphasis on keeping varieties just as they always have been. Because of the emphasis on obvious physical traits such as the size and color of the crop, the process of saving heirlooms could be preserving less diversity than we might think. But heirlooms do possess valuable traits worth preserving. Growing them allows individual gardeners to become part of the preservation process and helps increase awareness of the importance of diversity. Besides, partaking of the delicious bounty of heirlooms gives a great deal of pleasure to many

---

Farm parks such as John Bender's Mokelumne River Ranch in Thornton, California, are fun to visit and are a good source for animals for the family farm, such as these Nubian goats (not a rare breed). PHOTO BY DOROTHY H. PATENT

people. The network that has developed, thanks to organizations such as Seed Savers Exchange, is crucial to the success of the goal of preserving diversity.

Each farm park may only preserve a limited number of rare breeds, but their combined effect on preservation and on public education can be profound. Farm parks allow ordinary citizens the opportunity to purchase unusual animals that can thrive on small homesteads, and they can give their visitors a special appreciation for the wonderful diversity created through the cooperation of humans and nature during the domestication process.

Allowing Evolution to Flourish

Storing genes in banks isn't the only way to preserve valuable genes so that traits such as disease resistance will be available when needed by plant breeders. A little-known way of allowing evolution to proceed in harmony with the ever-evolving nature of disease organisms and with changes in climate and atmospheric conditions does exist and has proved highly productive over the years, at least with one crop.

In 1929, Dr. Harry Harlan mixed the seeds for several dozen land races of barley in a big bag and then planted them in a large plot at the University of California, Davis. The field was grown in the same way as commercial barley plantings, but all the seed was collected, with no selection by the grower. Every year, from then until now, the barley has been grown and harvested. Seeds from the parental stocks and from each year's harvest were preserved in storage, creating a record now more than sixty years long of the evolution of this barley mixture. In 1989, Dr. R. W.

Allard summarized findings over the years and analyzed the seeds from the ever-evolving plot to see what changes had occurred through time.

He found that the barley stayed genetically diverse for a number of traits, including external appearance of the plants, the amount of grain produced, and disease resistance. Through the years, damage due to disease was small. The levels of infestation varied depending on changes in the environment, but no disease ever reached epidemic proportions, even in years when commercial plantings were devastated. Allard's results show great promise for this method as another way of preserving useful genetic diversity.

The incidence of all barley diseases in the mixture dropped steadily over the years as the barley recombined genes and developed new mutations. None of the parent land races planted in 1929 were resistant to all three of the most important barley diseases in California's Central Valley—powdery mildew, net blotch, and four different races of scald. After forty-five years—less than an instant by evolutionary standards—more than a third (36 percent) of the plants carried three resistances and almost as many (32 percent) were quadruply resistant. Six percent were resistant to five or six of the diseases and scald strains.

For a modern barley breeder who wants to develop highly disease-resistant varieties, such plants are a godsend. Tapping into the barley that has been allowed to evolve would be much more useful than acquiring seed of the original parental strains from a gene bank and trying to combine the selection of resistances into one variety. Twenty-nine or more different genes involved in disease resistance existed in the various parental strains, resulting in millions of possible genetic combinations. A breeder would have a hard time even knowing where to start the process of bringing together the best possible combinations of genes through crosses among all those land races. But over the years, nature has painlessly accomplished that task with minimal input of time and effort by humans. Fortunately, barley breeders have taken advantage of evolution's work and utilized lines from the Davis plots in their efforts to develop the best barley possible.

This method of creating "composite crosses" of many land races with a variety of useful traits and growing them on "mass selection plots" is being utilized more and more frequently with crops besides barley. Beginning in 1934, similar plots using seed from sixteen inbred strains of corn were established in Iowa. As with barley, seed from these corn plots has proved very useful to breeders looking for disease resistance, yield improvement, and other traits.

Saving the Wild

Just as we need to preserve domesticated breeds on farms (not just as frozen embryos) and cultivated varieties as heirlooms in gardens and dynamically evolving species in mass selection plots (not just in gene banks), so must we preserve the wild relatives of our domesticated animals and cultivated plants in their natural homes where they can continue to survive and evolve along with the rest of the changing, living world. As the world's human population grows, wild places disappear. The rain forest is being chopped down to make room for agriculture, destroying the homes of countless wild plants and animals. Wetlands are drained and filled to make places for homes and shopping malls. Most of the losers are not close relatives of domesticated and cultivated species, but they also have value to the planet that is impossible to measure. The preservation of wild relatives cannot be separated from saving the habitat of wild plants and wildlife in general.

Countries around the world have established parks and preserves with the stated goal of protecting wild places. Unfortunately, many of these are just "paper parks" with no enforcement of preservation and no preservation plans. People may continue to farm and log in such places, destroying plant life and habitat, and animals may be shot for food or other products they can provide. Unless countries put money into protecting their parks, biodiversity will continue to disappear at the same alarming rate no matter how much green appears on the map.

Private organizations also participate in saving wildlands. The Nature Conservancy (TNC) is a leader in this field. TNC avoids political battles and quietly acquires land where rare species reside. When it believes the government can do a good job of preserving the land, TNC may deed the property over so it can concentrate its energies on further preservation.

Sustainable Agriculture

While American agriculture is producing enormous quantities of food at prices envied around the world, it does so at a great price to the future of both agriculture and the environment. The herbicides, pesticides, and fertilizers applied to the countless millions of acres devoted to crops are endangering our lakes, rivers, and groundwater.

Without healthy water supplies, we cannot be healthy people. Public concern about agricultural pollution is growing. A 1993 survey found that 71 percent of people polled were "very concerned" about fertilizers and pesticides getting into the water supply, and 68 percent were very concerned about the effects of pesticides in the food supply on the health of children. A majority also felt farmers should farm organically, that the government should encourage farmers to use fewer chemicals, and that people should be told the kinds of chemicals used to produce the foods in the supermarket.

In addition to polluting the water and adding potentially dangerous chemicals to the food supply, modern farm practices damage the land. The soil on our farms becomes poorer and poorer each season, with less and less vital organic matter and smaller and smaller amounts of the trace elements plants need to grow properly and to provide an abundant harvest. The system as it is today cannot go on forever, and more and more farmers are beginning to realize that more sustainable techniques need to be implemented.

The concept of sustainable agriculture is quite simple: use the land in such a way as to keep it healthy so that future generations will be able to obtain abundant harvests from it and so that the environment is not degraded. Sustainable agriculture also involves treating farm animals humanely.

A number of techniques can help make agriculture sustainable. A common practice for large commercial farms is to leave the land bare for months at a time between crop plantings. Herbicides may be applied to the ground to keep weeds from growing. But barren land is highly susceptible to loss of topsoil due to wind erosion. Every year, American farms lose millions of tons of topsoil to the wind. Instead of leaving fields fallow, sustainable agricultural practice would mean planting the ground with a "cover crop." Some of the best cover crops belong to the pea family, which has the ability to take nitrogen from the air and convert it into a form plants can use. By planting a cover crop, which is then plowed under before planting the crop to be harvested, a farmer can add nitrogen and organic matter to the soil while protecting the topsoil from erosion.

Integrated pest management (IPM) is another sustainable technique. Instead of applying massive amounts of pesticides, IPM relies on a variety of methods to control pests. Many pests can be controlled simply through the timing of planting. For example, certain flies lay their eggs in the soil in plantings of radishes or carrots. But the flies are active only early in the season. By planting after the flies are gone, a carrot farmer can avoid the pests without spending money on pesticides or investing the time, gasoline, and equipment involved in applying them to the crop. Predators such as ladybugs that eat some pests are available commercially. These predators don't kill off all the pests, but they can help control their numbers and reduce pest damage to the crop. Intercropping—planting more than one kind of crop in a field—can also discourage pests. When crops are mixed, fewer pests are able to find their target food.

Sustainable agriculture takes more knowledge and commitment from farmers than current common commercial practices. It also takes more work and careful planning. But it results in better soil and healthier produce and can end up reducing a farmer's up-front costs considerably. If a farmer is committed to farming organically—without chemical fertilizers, pesticides, or herbicides—the resulting produce can bring a premium price on the market.

The national government is showing some interest in the concept of sustainable agriculture. In 1991, the U.S. Department of Agriculture allocated $6.7 million for sustainable agriculture. But that same year, the USDA invested $150 million in biotechnology. We still have a long way to go to support healthy use of the land.

Using Biotechnology to Advantage

The same biotechnology that breeders are exploiting to increase genetic uniformity in domesticated animals can be harnessed to preserve diversity. Semen from rare breed bulls can be collected and distributed widely just as easily as that from bulls of common breeds. The splitting and cloning of embryos from rare breeds or the declining lines of more common breeds would not increase diversity significantly. Nonetheless, these techniques could be of value. Through cloning, multiples of rare gene combinations could be stored in different places as backups, reducing the chance they would disappear forever. Clones could allow scientists to test the suitability of the same genetic constitution to different environments and allow different breeders to utilize individuals with identical genetic makeup.

Up to now, the splitting and cloning of embryos has

not reached the stage where it can be used reliably. But with time, the methods will improve. We can hope that those who work to preserve diversity as well as those who strive for uniformity will take advantage of these techniques.

Maintaining Tradition

Methods of traditional agriculture have proved their value over time. For hundreds of generations, Native Americans in North, Central, and South America planted their gardens of mixed varieties of corn, beans, and squash. Their methods produced enough food to support the large cities of the Maya and the Aztecs as well as farms and villages in the countryside. Today, people are trying to find ways of encouraging the continuation of traditional agriculture not only in the Americas but on other continents as well.

Such projects have been initiated in scattered locations in Mexico and Central and South America. If farming systems based on traditional methods can be maintained in the centers of diversity of the world's crop plants, much of the useful diversity could be preserved while allowing the crops to evolve in tandem with their pests and diseases and with the expected changes in the planet's atmosphere and climate brought about by human activities. One project in Mexico combines growing vegetables and raising animals with recycling organic materials to maintain rich, healthy soils. In addition to raising the traditional crops of beans, squash, and corn for local consumption, the project involves growing cash crops such as Swiss chard, cabbage, and chili peppers.

Sharing the Wealth

It seems only right that the countries where diversity prevails be financially compensated for the genes extracted
from their land races and used by the multinational seed
companies to make big money. Rural Advancement Foundation International estimates that agriculture in developed countries gains $5 billion from Third World genetic
resources each year. In 1991, the American pharmaceutical
firm Merck and Co. struck a deal with the National Biodiversity Institute of Costa Rica. The institute provides
Merck with samples of Costa Rican plants and animals,
and Merck tests the samples for possible commercial uses.
Merck has the right to patent any products it develops,
but it has already given the Biodiversity Institute more
than a million dollars and will pay royalties on any products it develops. While Merck is primarily interested in
potential pharmaceuticals, similar agreements might be
worked out between seed companies and the governments
of countries with abundant crop and wild relative diversity within their borders. The Merck deal has been widely
criticized for providing too little compensation. But at
least now there is a model that can be studied by other
governments and companies.

Developed as well as developing nations have recog-
nized the need for cooperation in exploiting biological
diversity for human benefit. During the United Nations
Conference on Environment and Development in Rio de
Janeiro in June 1992, a treaty giving guidelines for this
process (the United Nations Convention on Biological
Diversity) was hammered out. While many countries

signed the treaty at that time, the United States refused to do so. It has since been signed by the U.S. under the Clinton administration and went into effect on December 29, 1993.

Among the treaty's provisions are recommendations that biological diversity be preserved both in the wild and in gene banks or some other form of managed preservation, preferably in the countries of origin. The treaty calls for the exploration and mapping of biodiversity, specifically mentioning the wild relatives of domesticated animals and cultivated plant species. It affirms the principle that the benefits derived from biodiversity, such as disease-resistant genes, should be shared between the nation from which the resource came and the party that exploits it, such as a seed breeder.

Ultimately, the world's industries, agricultural systems, and governments must all cooperate to find a sustainable way of feeding the world's ever-growing population without destroying the land upon which we all depend. We need to do our best to utilize and perfect every approach in order to be successful, which means refining seed banks, heirloom seed preservation, mass selection plots, farm parks, zoos, and sustainable and traditional methods of agriculture.

Ultimately, we all depend on one another for survival. Our planet is small. Humans and the natural world are intimately interconnected, and these mutual dependencies are especially striking in any agricultural endeavor. We must participate in a generous give-and-take with nature and her bounty or suffer very painful consequences.

ACRONYMS

ALBC   American Livestock Breeds Association

CGIAR   Consultative Group on International Agricultural
            Research

EPA   Environmental Protection Agency

GRIN   Germplasm Resources Information Network

IPM   Integrated Pest Management

NAFEX   North American Fruit Explorers

NSSL   National Seed Storage Laboratory

PBR   Plant Breeders' Rights

PI Number   Plant Introduction Number

RAFI   Rural Advancement Foundation International

TNC   The Nature Conservancy

UPOV   Union for the Protection of New Varieties of Plants

USDA   United States Department of Agriculture

GLOSSARY

Adaptation: In biology, the process by which a species becomes suited to survival in its environment over a number of generations. The better-suited individuals in each generation are likely to leave more offspring than less well adapted ones. In this way, the species as a whole becomes suited, or adapted, to the environment in which it lives. Adaptation can also refer to a well-adapted trait.

Alleles: The different forms of a particular gene that determine the variations of a trait. For example, different alleles for a hair color gene produce different colors of hair.

Cell: The smallest unit of living material of which all living things are composed. Cells consist of living matter and a nucleus, surrounded by a membrane. Some organisms, such as bacteria and protozoa, have just one cell. Others, such as humans, have millions or billions of cells.

Cell nucleus: The central or main part of the cell, containing the chromosomes.

Chromosome: A roughly rod-shaped structure inside the cell nucleus carrying the genes that determine the traits of the organism.

Cross-pollination: The process by which the pollen from one plant pollinates the flowers of another plant.

Crossing-over: The process by which the two matching chromosomes exchange pieces, resulting in the reshuffling of their genes.

Cryostorage: Keeping items such as seeds at very low temperatures (−256°F, −160°C or lower) in order to prolong their survival.

Cultivar: A variety of a cultivated plant. Butterhead and romaine are cultivars of lettuce, for example.

Dominant allele: An allele that expresses itself when only one copy is present.

Evolution: The process by which, over time, living things change genetically and separate into different species.

Fertilization: The joining of the sperm of the male with the egg of the female to produce a new organism.

Gene: The individual unit of heredity that controls the expression of traits in an organism, such as size, color, and blood type.

Gene bank: A place where seeds and other reproducible parts of plants are kept to help preserve genetic diversity.

Gene pool: The total of all the genes in the members of a particular population of organisms that are able to reproduce.

Genetic diversity: The range of physical traits of a species. The greater the genetic diversity of a species, the better able it is to adapt to changes in the environment.

Genetic engineering: The changing of an organism's genetic makeup by scientists to produce more desirable traits in that organism.

Genetic recombination: The mixing of genes that occurs during the production of egg and sperm cells and during the process of fertilization.

Germplasm: The hereditary material passed from one generation to the next.

Green Revolution: The increased development during the 1960s and 1970s of new, high-yielding varieties of basic crops such as rice to feed the rapidly growing human population.

Herbicides: Chemicals used to kill weeds.

Hybrid: An organism that results from the crossing of two genetically different parents. In plant breeding, the parents are members of carefully inbred strains of the same species. A hybrid may also be an individual resulting from the crossing of two different species.

Hybrid vigor: The strong, healthy growth and production of organisms that have great diversity within their genes, usually resulting from the crossing of two genetically different inbred strains.

Inbreeding: The repeated mating of closely related organisms of a particular species that results in genetic similarity. In plant breeding, related plants with desirable traits are inbred for generations until they have little genetic diversity. Then two different inbred strains are crossed to produce vigorous hybrids.

Land races: Plant varieties that have adapted over time to the conditions under which they grow. Land races are often a great source of important traits such as disease resistance.

Miracle varieties: The carefully bred, high-yielding varieties developed during the Green Revolution. Most miracle varieties are hybrids.

Mutations: The changes in genes that produce the differences in organisms, such as length of hair, disease resistance, or tolerance to heat.

Open-pollinated varieties: Varieties of plants that pollinate themselves, without the help of humans. Unlike hybrid varieties, open-pollinated varieties are generally similar to their parent plants.

Planting out: The process in which seeds kept in seed banks are planted and grown to maturity periodically for renewal. Planting out is necessary because seeds lose their vigor with time and can die in storage.

Pollen: The tiny powdery particles produced by the male parts of flowers that contain a plant's sperm.

Pollination: The process of fertilization of the female part of the flower by the male part, or pollen.

Recessive allele: An allele that expresses itself only when present in both copies of a gene.

Sexual reproduction: Reproduction in which new combinations of genes result from the mixture of genes from two parents.

Stigma: The female part of the flower onto which pollen sticks during pollination.

Tubers: The swollen underground stems of plants such as potatoes that lie dormant during the winter and sprout to produce new plants in the spring. People harvest some tubers for food.

BIBLIOGRAPHY

In writing this book I used a wide variety of resources. Many of the books listed are symposium volumes containing articles by different authors. Not all resources are included; for example, some information was obtained from newsletters of organizations involved in preserving diversity and from personal interviews.

Allard, R. W. "The Genetics of Host-pathogen Coevolution: Implications for Genetic Resource Conservation." *The Journal of Heredity* 81 (1990): 1–6.

Board on Agriculture, National Research Council. *Managing Global Genetic Resources: Agricultural Crop Issues and Policies.* Washington, D.C.: National Academy Press, 1993.

Board on Science and Technology for International Development, National Research Council. *Little-Known Asian Animals with a Promising Economic Future.* Washington, D.C.: National Academy Press, 1983.

————. *Microlivestock: Little-Known Small Animals with a Promising Economic Future.* Washington, D.C.: National Academy Press, 1991.

Committee on Managing Global Genetic Resources: Agricultural Imperatives. Board on Agriculture, National Research Council. *Managing Global Genetic Resources: Livestock.* Washington, D.C.: National Academy Press, 1993.

Dodds, John H., ed. *In Vitro Methods for Conservation of Plant Genetic Resources.* New York: Chapman and Hall, 1991.

Falk, Donald A., and Kent E. Holsinger, eds. *Genetics and Conservation of Rare Plants.* New York: Oxford University Press, 1991.

Ford-Lloyd, B. V., and M. T. Jackson. "Biotechnology and Methods of Conservation of Plant Genetic Resources." *Journal of Biotechnology* 17 (1991): 247–256.

Gasser, Charles S., and Robert T. Fraley. "Genetically Engineering Plants for Crop Improvement." *Science* 244 (1989): 1293–1299.

Glaeser, Bernhard. *The Green Revolution Revisited: Critique and Alternatives.* London: Allen and Unwin, 1987.

Goodman, M. M. "Genetic and Germ Plasm Stocks Worth Conserving." *The Journal of Heredity* 81 (1990): 11–16.

Hawkes, J. G. *The Potato: Evolution, Biodiversity, and Genetic Resources.* Washington, D.C.: Smithsonian Institution Press, 1990.

Hobbelink, Henk. *Biotechnology and the Future of World Agriculture: The Fourth Resource.* Atlantic Highlands, New Jersey: Zed Books Ltd., 1991.

Holden, J. A. W., and J. T. Williams, eds. *Crop Genetic Resources: Conservation and Evaluation.* London: Allen and Unwin, 1984.

Hyland, H. L. "History of U.S. Plant Introduction." *Environmental Review* 4 (1977): 26–33.

Iltis, Hugh, H. J. F. Doebley, R. Guzmán, and B. Pazy. "*Zea diploperennis* (Gramineaé): A New Teosinte from Mexico." *Science* 203 (1979): 186–188.

Murty, B. R., and Melak H. Mengesha. "World Germplasm Collections and Their Potential in Crop Productivity." *Indian Journal of Agricultural Sciences* 60 (1990): 787–792.

Plucknett, Donald L., et al. *Gene Banks and the World's Food.* Princeton, New Jersey: Princeton University Press, 1987.

Pursel, Vernon G., et al. "Genetic Engineering of Livestock." *Science* 244 (1989): 1281–1288.

Redclift, Michael. *Development and the Environmental Crisis: Red or Green Alternatives?* New York: Methuen, 1984.

Simmonds, N. W., ed. *Evolution of Crop Plants.* New York: Longman, 1976.

Tinker, Catherine J. "Introduction to Biological Diversity: Law, Institutions, and Science." *Buffalo Journal of International Law* 1 (1994): 1–27.

USDA Agricultural Research Service. Program Aid No. 1470. *Seeds for Our Future: The United States National Plant Germplasm System.* 1990.

Wilson, E. O., ed. *Biodiversity.* Washington, D.C.: National Academy Press, 1988.

Wood, J. D., and A. V. Fisher, eds. *Reducing Fat in Meat Animals.* New York: Elsevier Applied Science, 1990.

Zeven, A. C., and A. M. van Harten, eds. *Broadening the Genetic Base of Crops. Proceedings of the Conference, Wageningen, Netherlands, 3–7 July, 1978.* Wageningen: Centre for Agricultural Publishing and Documentation, 1979.

ORGANIZATIONS OF INTEREST

American Livestock Breeds Conservancy (formerly American Minor Breeds Conservancy), P.O. Box 477, Pittsboro, NC 27312.
  Offers a number of services, including a newsletter, book sales, and registries for owners of minor breeds; membership available.
Native Seeds/Search, 2509 North Campbell Avenue, No. 325, Tucson, AZ 85719.
  Focuses on preserving traditional North American crops, especially those grown by Native Americans. Maintains a seed bank and sells seeds to gardeners (catalog: $1.00).
The Nature Conservancy, 1815 North Lynn Street, Arlington, VA 22209.
  Buys critical wildlife habitats and sets up conservation easements to protect habitats.
Rare Breeds Survival Trust Ltd., Fourth Street, National Agricultural Centre, Kenilworth, Warks CV8 2LG, UK.
  Works to conserve rare breeds by providing support to those who raise rare breeds and services such as semen banks; membership available.
Rural Advancement Foundation International—USA (RAFI—USA), P.O. Box 655, Pittsboro, NC 27312.
  Works on preserving diversity and helping rural communities around the world in a number of ways, including through the United Nations; publishes a variety of materials including a wall map, "The Seed Map, Dinner on the Third World," which illustrates the centers of diversity around the world; membership available.

Seed Savers Exchange, Rural Route 3, Box 239, Decorah, IA 52101.
Provides network for gardeners wanting to grow heirloom varieties, including catalog of thousands of rare and unusual vegetables; has numerous publications; membership available.

Seeds of Change, 621 Old Santa Fe Trail, No. 10, Santa Fe, NM 87501.
Offers organically grown seeds of heirloom and unusual vegetables and acts as a consultant on organic farming (catalog: $5.00).

SUGGESTED READING

BOOKS

Alderson, Lawrence. *The Chance to Survive.* London: Christopher Helm, 1990. (Available through the American Livestock Breeds Conservancy.)

A British book about all aspects of endangerment of rare breeds and their importance.

Broom, Donald M., ed. *All the World's Animals: Farmed Animals.* New York: Torstar Books, 1986.

Part of a series on animals of the world, with illustrations and descriptions of many livestock breeds.

Doyle, Jack. *Altered Harvest: Agriculture, Genetics, and the Fate of the World's Food Supply.* New York: Viking, 1985.

How reduced genetic diversity can endanger our food supply.

Fowler, Cary, and Pat Mooney. *Shattering: Food, Politics, and the Loss of Genetic Diversity.* Tucson: University of Arizona Press, 1990.

The authors present powerful arguments for why we need to be concerned about both the loss of diversity and the concentration of food-related businesses in the hands of a few huge corporations.

Fussell, Betty. *The Story of Corn.* New York: Alfred A. Knopf, 1992.

Everything you ever wanted to know about this vitally important world crop, from folklore to science.

Harlan, Jack R. *Crops & Man.* 2d ed. Madison, Wisconsin: American Society of Agronomy, Inc., 1992.

A scientific but readable account of the history of humankind's relationship with domesticated plants.

Hawkes, J. G. *The Diversity of Crop Plants.* Cambridge, Massachusetts:

Harvard University Press, 1983.

A readable book about crop plant diversity and its importance.

Nabhan, Gary Paul. *Enduring Seeds: Native American Agriculture and Wild Plant Conservation.* San Francisco: North Point Press, 1989.

A beautifully written book about the importance of genetic variability, especially to Native American societies.

Teitel, Martin. *Rain Forest in Your Kitchen: The Hidden Connection between Extinction and Your Supermarket.* Washington, D.C.: Island Press, 1992.

Information on disappearance of wild species and cultivated varieties and how shopping behavior can affect the preservation of diversity; includes information on both animals and plants.

Viola, Herman J., and Carolyn Margolis. *Seeds of Change: A Quincentennial Commemoration.* Washington, D.C.: Smithsonian Institution Press, 1991.

A celebration of the New World's contributions to agriculture, including corn.

Visser, Margaret. *Much Depends on Dinner.* New York: Collier Books, 1986.

A set of entertaining and informative essays on a number of important foods including corn, chicken, and rice.

Whitlock, Ralph. *Rare Breeds: The Vulnerable Survivors.* New York: Van Nostrand Reinhold Co., 1980.

A compendium of rare livestock breeds and their uses.

MAGAZINE ARTICLES

Creasy, Rosalind. "Three Sisters of Life: Squash, Beans and Corn in the Native American Garden. *Harrowsmith,* September/October 1988: 81–87.

Information on the three basic Native American crops.

Drew, Lisa. "In Search of the Barnyard Ark." *National Wildlife,* December–January 1991: 42–48.

Endangered breeds and efforts to save them.

Feature Section: "Who Decides What You Eat?" Co-op America Quarterly, Spring 1992: 10–21.

Includes an article on America's meat industry, another on the problems of modern biotechnology and consolidation of seed houses with agricultural chemical businesses, a "What You Can Do" list, and a list of resources on related topics.

MacFadyen, J. Tevere. "The Zookeeper's Example." *Harrowsmith*, July/August 1987: 60–68.
Saving Devon cattle and other rare breeds.

Raloff, Janet. "Corn's Slow Path to Stardom: Archaeologists Rewrite the History of Maize and New World Civilization." *Science News* 143 (1993): 248–250.
Recent information on the history of corn.

Rhoades, Robert E. "The Incredible Potato." *National Geographic*, May 1982: 668–94.
Fascinating information about the history, variation, and uses of potatoes.

——. "The World's Food Supply at Risk." *National Geographic*, April 1991: 74–105.
How loss of genetic diversity threatens humankind.

Shell, Ellen Ruppel. "Seeds in the Bank Could Stave Off Disaster on the Farm." *Smithsonian*, January 1990: 94–105.
How seed banks can help stave off loss of diversity in crop plants.

Special Section: Biotechnology & Ecology. The Amicus Journal, Spring 1993.
Includes five articles on biotechnology and the problems of breeding uniformity. *The Amicus Journal* is published by the Natural Resources Defense Council.

Wickelgren, Ingrid. "Please Pass the Genes." *Science News* 136 (1989):120–124.
Health concerns about genetically engineered foods.

INDEX

cabbage family, 112
Calgene, 65–66
cattle, 81–83, 86–89
  Angus, 92
  beef, 86, 91, 92, 101; *see also*
    specific breeds
  Charolais, 88
  Chianina, 87
  dairy, 86, 91, 92, 103; *see also*
    specific breeds
  disease resistance in, 81
  dwarf West African shorthorn,
    87
  embryo, splitting of, 101–2
  English longhorn, 88
  Eringer, 88
  Galloway, 75, 81–82
  Guernsey, 138
  Hereford, 92
  Holstein-Friesian, 88, 91,
    103
  horns, 86–87
  Madura, 88
  Maine Anjou, 87
  origin of, 86
  Piedmontese, 22
  shorthorn, 88
  Texas longhorn, 82–83
  uniformity in, 102
  uses of, 86, 87–88
  Western type, 86
  West Highlands, 81
  zebu type, 86
cell, 159
  nucleus of, 159
Central America, 7, 97, 112, 124,
  153
chickens, 93–96, 101

broiler, 92, 93, 94, 95–96
Cornish, 96
Dominique, 96
egg-layers, 92, 93–95
loss of diversity in, 92, 95
normal behavior of, 93–94
White Leghorn, 95
White Plymouth Rock, 96
China, 123
chromosomes, 5–6, 159
  corn, 23
Ciba-Geigy, 63
cloning of embryos, 101–2, 152
coffee, 19
cold storage, of seeds, 110
composite crosses, 147–48
corn, 5–6, 15–16, 23–28, 30,
  57–58, 119, 148, 153
  African, 19
  dent, 25
  disease resistance in, 19
  flint, 25
  flour, 25
  Golden Cross Bantam, 27
  Hopi blue flour, 27
  male-sterile gene, 17, 19
  origin of, 23–25, 112
  pollination of, 16
  popcorn, 25
  seeds, 23, 109–110
  silks of, 16
  sweet, 25
  syrup, 65
  Tarahumara blue flint, 27
  tassels, 16
  uses of, 25–27
  variations in, 25
  varieties, 26–28

maize; *see* corn
Mangelsdorf, Paul, 24
mass selection plots, 146–48
McDonalds, 33
McNeal, Lyle, 78
meat
  lean, 77, 84–85
  marbling, 22
medical research, 78–79, 80
Merck and Co., 154
Mexico, 7, 17, 23, 27, 42, 97, 112, 124, 153
midwestern states, U.S., 18, 19, 25, 127
miracle varieties, 43–44, 161
  growing, 44
mithan, 143
Mokelumne River Ranch, 76–81, 138, 141, 144
monoculture, 48
mutations, 6–7, 161

Nabhan, Gary, 27
NAFEX; *see* North American Fruit Explorers
National Germplasm Resource Laboratory, 113
National Plant Germplasm Quarantine Center, 113–14
National Seed Storage Laboratory (NSSL), 109, 111, 113, 114–16, 129
  seed samples, handling of, 114–15
Native Americans, 25, 57–58, 132, 153; *see also* Hopi Indians, Navajo Indians
Native Seeds/SEARCH, 131–32

Nature Conservancy, The (TNC), 149
Navajo Indians, 25, 77–78
Near East, 123–24
Nicholas Turkey Breeding Farm, 99
nitrogen, liquid, 111
North American Fruit Explorers (NAFEX), 133–34
NSSL; *see* National Seed Storage Laboratory
nucleus, of cell, 6
nutrition, 58

Ochoa, Carlos, 36
oleic acid, 68
onions, 112
open-pollinated varieties, 161
Orange County, Calif., 13
Ott, Baptist, 127–28

Pakistan, 43
palm oil, 20
parks and preserves, problems with, 149
Patent Appeals, U.S. Board of, 69
patent law, 67–69
patenting genes, 66–71
  practical problems of, 67–71
  theoretical problems of, 67–68
PBR; *see* Plant Breeders' Rights
peaches, 112
  Oldmixon Free, 134
Peru, 5, 28, 32, 35
pesticides, 20, 44, 48, 63, 150, 151
Philippines, 42
  corn in, 17
  Green Revolution in, 47

University of California, Davis, 9, 146–47
Upjohn, 63
UPOV; *see* Union for the Protection of New Varieties of Plants
Urban, Tom, 64–65
USDA; *see* United States Department of Agriculture
U.S. National Plant Germplasm System, 112–13, 114

varieties; *see also* land races, plant breeding
  heirloom, 128–35
  open-pollinated, 51, 131
Vavilov Institute, 4, 108, 122, 123
Vavilov, Nikolai, 123–24

watermelon, Nancy, 129–30
water pollution, 48
Whealy, Kent, 127–28
wheat, 30, 43
whitefly, greenhouse, 13
Wichita Mountains Wildlife Refuge, 83
wool, 10, 76, 77, 78
World Potato Collection, 33, 37
World War II, 4

yak, 89
yakow, 89

zebras, 137
zoos, role in preserving diversity, 142

GREYHOUND INTERMEDIATE SCHOOL
805 GREYHOUND DR.
EATON RAPIDS, MI 48827